NOTHING TO FEAR

NOTHING TO FEAR

Lessons in Leadership from FDR

ALAN AXELROD

PORTFOLIO

PORTFOLIO
Published by the Penguin Group
Penguin Group (USA) Inc., 375 Hudson Street, New York, New York 10014, U.S.A.
Penguin Books Ltd, 80 Strand, London WC2R 0RL, England
Penguin Books Australia Ltd, 250 Camberwell Road,
Camberwell, Victoria 3124, Australia
Penguin Books Canada Ltd, 10 Alcorn Avenue, Toronto, Ontario, Canada M4V 3B2
Penguin Books India (P) Ltd, 11 Community Centre, Panchsheel Park,
New Delhi – 110 017, India
Penguin Books (N.Z.) Ltd, Cnr Rosedale and Airborne Roads,
Albany, Auckland, New Zealand
Penguin Books (South Africa) (Pty) Ltd, 24 Sturdee Avenue,
Rosebank, Johannesburg 2196, South Africa

Penguin Books Ltd, Registered Offices: 80 Strand, London WC2R 0RL, England

First published in 2003 by Portfolio, a member of Penguin Group (USA) Inc.

1   3   5   7   9   10   8   6   4   2

LIBRARY OF CONGRESS CATALOGING-IN-PUBLICATION DATA
Axelrod, Alan, 1952–
Nothing to fear : lessons in leadership from FDR / Alan Axelrod.
p.   cm.
Includes bibliograhical references and index.
ISBN 1-59184-014-7
1. Political leadership.   2. Roosevelt, Franklin D. (Franklin Delano), 1882–1945.
3. United States—Politics and government—1933–1945.   I. Title.
JC330.3.A95 2003b
973.917'092—dc21   2002193165

This book is printed on acid-free paper. ∞

Printed in the United States of America • Designed by Nancy Resnick

For Anita and Ian

Preface

ANOTHER GENERATION, ANOTHER RENDEZVOUS WITH DESTINY

Sooner or later every world leader is called upon to utter words that are supposed to ring with historic import. Some have a more profound grasp of history than others. Some just have a better ear for resonant phrases. And some, like Lincoln, Churchill, and Franklin Delano Roosevelt, possess both a quick and deep historic understanding *and* abundant gifts of eloquent self-expression.

No one who came of age in the 1930s and 1940s can forget FDR's observation on the hand history dealt to that generation. Stirring, his pronouncement is also strangely haunting, verging even on the mystical. "There is a mysterious cycle in human events," he declared in a speech to the 1936 Democratic National Convention. "To some generations much is given. Of other generations much is expected. This generation of Americans has a rendezvous with destiny."

The passage is both moving and memorable but until recently it would have seemed strictly a page out of history, applicable to a certain time, place, people, and set of circumstances, but with little if any connection to us—today.

Then, of course, "today" changed.

On September 11, 2001, our generation had its rendezvous with destiny. It arrived in the form of the first attack on American soil since Pearl Harbor, which had been hit on December 7, 1941, during the third term of Franklin Roosevelt.

The new attack in a new century brought with it many things:

the shock of thousands of lives lost, the fear of what would happen next, the deepening of an economic downturn. Yet with all this, it also brought a rebirth of patriotism, of solidarity with others, of compassion, of selflessness, and of courage, as well as a collective counting of blessings.

Instantly, in the wrenching wake of four terrible blows, we began to feel something of what that earlier generation, born of depression and forged in war, had felt. And if we now had a rendezvous with destiny, so the world of Franklin Roosevelt had a rendezvous with ours. In the bewildering mix of crisis and fear and hope, awash in media-borne images of destruction and rescue, the thoughts of many turned to leadership.

People said a lot of different things about September 11, 2001. But just about everybody said one thing: Reality had changed.

And that is where our rendezvous with FDR begins. For in the early 1930s Americans also faced a whole new reality, a reality of doom, doom animated by terror, what the incoming president nailed in his first inaugural address as "fear itself—nameless, unreasoning, unjustified terror which paralyzes needed efforts to convert retreat into advance."

The world of 1933 was undeniably terrifying, but what FDR understood was that the greatest terror of all, the "only thing we have to fear" was "fear itself." He understood as well that the way out of fear was through leadership—not the brute force laid on against populations by the dictators of Italy, Germany, and Soviet Russia, but, as he explained in his first inaugural, a leadership for a free people: "In every dark hour of our national life, a leadership of frankness and vigor has met with that understanding and support of the people themselves which is essential to victory. I am convinced that you will again give that support to leadership in these critical days."

It is an extraordinary statement. In a time of pain so acute that many Americans felt abandoned by America itself, FDR redefined the crisis not as somehow un-American but, on the contrary, quintessentially American. He pointed to a remarkable fact that many have observed before and since: Whenever America has faced genuine peril, a great leader has risen to the occasion. Think of the founding fathers; think of Andrew Jackson; think of Abraham Lincoln; of Woodrow Wilson; and of Franklin Roosevelt himself. Yet in this inaugural statement, FDR neither aggrandizes himself nor takes upon himself the entire burden of leadership; for neither the glory nor the load is solely his. He both charges and empowers the people, "convinced" of the "support" they will give "to leadership."

These are the words of a strong democratic leader. They promise more than hope—anyone can make that promise. Herbert Hoover repeatedly promised that "prosperity is just around the corner," as if prosperity were an old friend, temporarily absent and certain to return, and not something each of us must work to create for ourselves, both individually and as a people. FDR promised more than hope. He pledged leadership, a leadership built on restoring to the people their identity as Americans by empowering them with confidence, by charging them with self-determination, and, ultimately, by giving to them the tools they needed to fulfill that charge.

He led the transformation of a generation swept by worldwide poverty and world war into what Tom Brokaw has provocatively called the "greatest generation."

Faced with our own new reality, many of us wonder if we today can also become a great generation.

The truth is that it doesn't take catastrophe to produce greatness. The events of September 11, the facts of increased challenges and up-ticked anxiety amid deflated economic expectations, these things should above all serve to make us aware of what has always been reality, whether or not we always grasped it. Danger, crisis, risk, disappointment, fear, and loss are obstacles along every road, through every place, in every time, and in every business, profession, and field of endeavor. Leadership in 1933, in 2001, and beyond, begins with realizing that obstacles create opportunities for achievement, for success, and even for greatness.

Fear and the drift created by fear remain grave menaces when well-being, let alone limitless prosperity, cannot be thoughtlessly assumed or taken for granted. But if the proposition that adversity is just opportunity in a different suit of clothes strikes you as hollow, please read on. For the life and career of Franklin Roosevelt give this statement abundant substance. And it is our great fortune, as it was the great fortune of those who lived through another epoch of economic uncertainty and war, that we may learn from the example, the courage, the penetration, and the eloquence of Franklin Delano Roosevelt.

How to Use This Book

Nothing to Fear will inspire, encourage, and instruct. For the example of FDR moves the spirit, bolsters faith, and provides a wealth of practical leadership advice, tips, tactics, and strategies.

If you are looking for some rigid division between the "inspirational" passages and the "practical" bits in the example of Roosevelt, you will look in vain. One of the great hallmarks of FDR's leadership genius is the absence of visible seams between greathearted motives and hard-nosed politics. For FDR leadership was practical inspiration or inspired practicality. Take your pick; the two are impossible to separate, and you cannot tell where one leaves off and the other begins.

What you *will* find here is a collection of leadership lessons drawn from the public words of Franklin Roosevelt, beginning with his unsuccessful run for the vice presidency in 1920, moving through his terms as governor of New York, and across the entire twelve-year span of his presidency during an economic depression of unprecedented depth and duration, and during a war of unheard-of devastation and consequence.

The leadership lessons are arranged according to fourteen themes:

> Theme One: On Purpose and Principle
> Theme Two: On Hard Fact and Hard Responsibility
> Theme Three: On Credibility
> Theme Four: On Making Contact
> Theme Five: On Refusing Defeat
> Theme Six: On Plain Speech and Good Talk
> Theme Seven: On Preparation and Risk
> Theme Eight: On Change
> Theme Nine: On Motivation
> Theme Ten: On Making Everyone Count
> Theme Eleven: On Self-Interest and Self-Sacrifice
> Theme Twelve: On Confidence and Courage
> Theme Thirteen: On Knowledge and Self-Knowledge
> Theme Fourteen: On Progress and Prediction

The order of the themes does not reflect the chronology of Roosevelt's life and career, but is intended to build a coherent picture of FDR as a revealing model of leadership values, ideas, skills, traits, tactics, and strategies. Within each theme, however, the leadership lessons are deployed in chronological order. Those who want a time-ordered overview of Roosevelt's life and career may read the Introduction, "FDR: Who He Was, What He Faced, How He Led," and the Appendix, "An FDR Chronology."

If this book satisfies your interest in Franklin Delano Roosevelt, it has failed. In viewing FDR as a source of leadership lessons, it only begins to explore the man and his times. Please consult "Recommended Reading," at the back of the book.

Contents

Introduction

FDR: WHO HE WAS, WHAT HE FACED, HOW HE LED

Franklin Delano Roosevelt was born on January 30, 1882, into the privileged world of a patrician family ensconced in an estate at Hyde Park, New York. Raised mainly by a loving if sometimes suffocating mother, the young man came even more fully under her influence after his father, James Roosevelt, died in 1900, when Franklin was seventeen. The death of his father was the first crack in an otherwise seamless idyll of sheltered gentility. Through age fourteen, the boy had been schooled at home by governesses and tutors. From 1896 to 1900, he attended Groton School in Massachusetts. Although steeped in a tradition created by old American money, Groton was led at the time by Headmaster Endicott Peabody, who imparted to his charges not a sense of the perquisites of privilege, but an ethic of public service. He taught that wealth brought an outstanding debt to society, an obligation to create a better world. This lesson was not lost on Franklin Roosevelt.

From Groton young Roosevelt went on to Harvard, graduating in 1904 without having achieved any particular distinction. While he was a student there, he fell in love with Anna Eleanor Roosevelt, his fifth cousin once removed and the niece of Theodore Roosevelt. On March 17, 1905, they were married, and over the next eleven years the Roosevelts had five children (a sixth died in infancy): Anna (1906), James (1907), Elliott (1910), Franklin D., Jr. (1914), and John (1916).

In appearance, their marriage was no different from any other union in their social circle. Outwardly it was, if not blissful, both decorous and satisfactory. But in fact the marriage of Franklin and Eleanor was often troubled. For one thing, if Sara Delano Roosevelt was overbearing as a mother, she was downright dictatorial as a mother-in-law. Franklin's allegiance and affection were clearly divided between her and his wife; even more seriously, his passion was more than once diverted to other women.

Yet the marriage survived both Franklin's mother and Eleanor's discovery that her husband was having an affair with her own social secretary, Lucy Mercer. Indeed the marriage did much more than merely survive. Whatever its discontents, it was a profound union, at the deepest level distinctly different from conventional upper-crust marriages. Husband and wife functioned as a powerful team, emotionally, intellectually, and politically. Not only did Eleanor nurture the best that was within her husband, he in turn marveled at what she became. Shy, always self-conscious of her willowy stature, Eleanor matured into a woman of great wisdom, compassion, common sense, and energy. Early on she became a social activist, and it was her highly developed social conscience that guided Franklin's own.

Franklin Roosevelt attended Columbia University Law School until the spring of 1907, but decided not to pursue his degree after he passed the New York State bar examination and joined a leading Wall Street firm. Almost immediately he discovered that corporate law, although highly profitable, was distinctly unfulfilling and he habitually took up the cases no one else in the firm wanted: low-paying matters for "small" clients and pro bono work for the indigent.

With his social awareness heightened, and encouraged by Eleanor, he decided in 1910 to run for state senator on the Democratic ticket.

Roosevelt took to campaigning with natural vigor. He proved both tireless and charismatic, a distinctly political animal. He easily won the election, despite having run in a rock-ribbed Republican district. In the state house Roosevelt soon made a name for himself as a Progressive reformer and an opponent of the machine politics of New York's infamous Tammany Hall. If he was a natural politician, he was also a born leader, and his reformist leadership attracted attention far beyond New York State, laying the foundation of a national reputation. He built on his reputation by supporting, in 1912, the presidential candidacy of reform Democrat Woodrow Wilson.

Once Wilson was safely nominated, Roosevelt ran for reelection to the state senate, but his campaign was severely hampered when he contracted typhoid fever—a common though serious ailment at the time. Along with his ability to lead, Roosevelt had a talent for choosing supporters and allies. Louis Howe, his new principal adviser and aide, helped drive Roosevelt to victory despite the illness that curtailed his campaign. Howe and Roosevelt developed an intense mutual loyalty and a highly effective working relationship. Louis Howe would remain Roosevelt's most trusted adviser until Howe's death in 1936.

Although he had been reelected to another state senate term, Roosevelt accepted the offer of a subcabinet post in the administration of Woodrow Wilson. He became assistant secretary of the navy under Secretary of the Navy Josephus Daniels. The post was attractive mainly because of its national scope and it also allowed Roosevelt to deal with ships and naval matters, both of which he loved. Moreover this was the very job Eleanor's uncle Theodore Roosevelt had held a decade and a half earlier. Franklin Roosevelt saw it as a place of learning and a point of entry.

Roosevelt quickly showed himself to be far more dynamic than his boss, the aging and affable Daniels. The young Roosevelt became a passionate and practical advocate of war preparedness, the development of a big navy, and an active foreign policy. With the outbreak of World War I in Europe in July 1914, Roosevelt became an early supporter of U.S. entry into the conflict—a position that clashed mildly with the pacifist-leaning Daniels—and after the United States had gotten into the war, Roosevelt personally visited the front in 1918.

It was soon apparent that Roosevelt's greatest talent was his highly developed ability to deal with people on all levels and of every class: admirals, department bureaucrats, and the rank and file of shipyard labor unions. He was highly effective in opposing the collusive bidding and price-fixing practices of defense contractors, and he became a kind of ramrod for the Navy Department, the one administrator to whom everyone turned when they needed to get something done quickly and correctly.

In 1920 Roosevelt enthusiastically accepted nomination as the Democratic vice presidential candidate, running with the governor of Ohio, James M. Cox. Roosevelt was well aware that in the isolationist political atmosphere of postwar America, he and his running mate stood virtually no chance of victory against Republican Warren G. Harding and his promise of a "return to normalcy." But Roosevelt did not take a defeatist attitude, and he did not conduct a perfunctory campaign. Instead he regarded the run as a valuable opportunity to gain exposure, to express his ideas, and to hone his campaigning skills. The main fact was this: He loved to campaign.

After the inevitable defeat, Roosevelt returned to the practice of law, forming his own firm and becoming vice president of a financial enterprise.

Then life took a sharp turn.

In August 1921 while vacationing at the family compound in Campobello, Canada, Franklin Roosevelt contracted polio. The disease robbed him of the use of his legs and, most friends and associates concluded, would also rob him of any further political career. Sara Delano counseled her stricken son to return to Hyde Park to live out his life in genteel retirement, but Eleanor Roosevelt rose to the occasion, successfully helping her husband fight off both despair and the well-meaning defeatism of his mother.

With Eleanor's encouragement and support, Franklin emerged from the crucible of devastating disease stronger and, if anything, more optimistic and energetic than ever. His coming to terms with personal loss and his learning to triumph over it would inspire and instruct him throughout the rest of his public life as he led the nation through depression and war.

In 1924, while fighting toward recovery, Roosevelt discovered the medicinal waters of Warm Springs, Georgia. Bathing there gave him immediate relief and, he hoped, would help him eventually to regain some use of his legs. It was typical of Roosevelt that he wanted to extend this personal discovery to aid other polio victims. He quickly formed and financed the Warm Springs Foundation, designed to make the therapeutic effect of Warm Springs and places like it available to all who needed it.

The year 1924 also brought Roosevelt back into the public arena as he delivered an eloquent and attention-getting speech nominating Al Smith as the Democratic candidate for president. Four years later Roosevelt successfully ran for governor of New York, a remarkable victory in an otherwise Republican year.

Roosevelt was elected to two terms as governor, battling a majority Republican legislature to push through many Progressive measures, including a program of reforestation, state-supported old-age pensions and unemployment insurance, labor legislation, and the public development of electric power. With the deepening of the Great Depression in 1931, during his second term, Roosevelt became the first governor in the nation to create an effective state relief administration. He put social worker Harry Hopkins in charge of the agency. Later Hopkins would join Louis Howe as one of President Roosevelt's closest confidants and advisers.

It was during his tenure as governor that Roosevelt created the

Fireside Chat, an unprecedented use of the still-new medium of radio to broadcast informal addresses directly to the American people. Direct communication with the public and an ability to create common cause became Roosevelt hallmarks, and the Fireside Chat would be a mainstay of the Roosevelt governorship and later of his presidency, helping to carry the nation through multiple crises.

In part as a result of the Fireside Chats, and because of the demonstrable economic relief brought by his Progressive agenda, Roosevelt was reelected as governor in 1930 by 750,000 votes, the largest margin in state history. During his gubernatorial administration, Roosevelt, always searching for innovative solutions to problems associated with the Depression, enlisted what he called a "brain trust," a band of Columbia University professors who collaborated on creating programs to fight the hard times. Many of these individuals would be carried over into his presidency and would be instrumental in formulating the New Deal.

In 1932 Roosevelt was nominated as the Democratic candidate for president. Always an innovator, he shattered precedent by flying to the convention to accept the nomination in person. "I pledge you," he declared to the delegates, "I pledge myself, to a new deal for the American people."

The "new deal" Roosevelt proposed was vast in scope and included federal spending for relief and public works, a plan to curb the agricultural overproduction that was depressing farm prices, a policy of conservation of environmental resources, a program to generate public power, a system to provide old-age pensions and unemployment insurance, a policy to regulate the stock exchange, and the repeal of prohibition. By a wide margin Roosevelt defeated Herbert Hoover, the Republican president many blamed (unjustly) for the Depression and many others reproached (with considerable justification) for doing too little to alleviate its effects.

Franklin Delano Roosevelt was inaugurated on March 4, 1933, at the nadir of the economic crisis, when some 15 million Americans found themselves unemployed. The failure of banks and other financial institutions had created widespread panic, which in turn brought about the collapse of even more banks. Roosevelt entered this dismal and dangerous picture by projecting an image of realistic confidence and optimism. His assertion in his inaugural address that "the only thing we have to fear is fear itself—nameless, unreasoning, unjustified terror," rang true precisely because he promised leadership, pledging to do far more than merely stand by as the Depression deepened. He would, he told the American people, obtain from Congress "the one remaining instrument to meet the crisis—broad executive power to wage a war against the emergency, as great as the power that would be given to me if we were in fact invaded by a foreign foe."

Almost immediately on taking office, Roosevelt declared a bank holiday to stave off a panic run on the financial institutions that were still functioning. Then he called Congress into emergency session. During the first hundred days of his administration, FDR introduced a sweeping program of relief measures. He took the nation off the gold standard, a step that offered some relief to debtors and exporters. He prevailed on Congress to appropriate $500 million in federal relief grants to state and local agencies. Under Harry Hopkins he created the Federal Emergency Relief Administration (FERA), the Civil Works Administration (CWA), the Civilian Conservation Corps (CCC), the Home Owners Loan Corporation (HOLC), and the Public Works Administration (PWA). The CCC employed more than 2.5 million young men in conservation work, the HOLC furnished emergency assistance to mortgagors and homeowners, enabling them to avoid foreclosure, and the PWA created great public works projects. These and other measures not only provided immediate relief to the desperate but generally restored hope among those hardest hit by the Depression. Without such measures many believed the nation would have plunged into civil insurrection or even outright revolution.

The New Deal was structured on a vast and all-encompassing scale. In addition to emergency relief, it included a program of longer range reform. The Federal Deposit Insurance Corporation (FDIC) insured bank deposits, an important safeguard against bank runs. The Securities and Exchange Commission (SEC) inaugurated the regulation of the stock exchanges, a safeguard against the kinds of practices that had contributed to the sudden collapse of the markets in 1929. The Tennessee Valley Authority (TVA) built great multipurpose dams to control floods and generate cheap hydroelectric power. Two agencies of special importance were the National Recovery Administration (NRA) and the Agricultural Adjustment Administration (AAA). The NRA provided incentives to management and labor to establish codes of fair competition within each industry, codes that included equitable pricing and production policies, collective bargaining, minimum wages, and maximum hours. The AAA sought to raise farm prices by setting production quotas approved by farmers in referenda and subsidizing farmers who stayed within the quotas.

Historians and economists continue to debate the efficacy of the New Deal. Certainly it did not, of itself, end the Great Depression. But it did provide quick relief, emergency aid, and, most important, longer term hope. FDR revealed himself to be innovative, flexible, determined, and compassionate. Outgoing, eloquent, and communicative, he kept the nation informed through frequent press conferences, speeches, and Fireside Chats. He was accepted overwhelmingly as a genuine leader whose charisma was irresistible and whose optimism was not only inspiring but entirely plausible.

The leadership task Roosevelt faced was supremely difficult, not just from an emotional and economic perspective but ideologically as well. He had to navigate a perilous course between preserving democracy, capitalism, and a free market economy on the one hand, and providing needed intervention, support, and control on the other. In 1935 FDR ushered through Congress three of his most sweeping initiatives: the Works Progress Administration (WPA), which employed millions in work relief programs; the Wagner Act, which set up the National Labor Relations Board (NLRB) and thereby guaranteed labor the right to bargain collectively on equal terms with management; and social security, which provided for federal payment of old-age pensions and for federal-state cooperation in support of unemployment compensation and relief for the blind and the disabled and for dependent children.

That the public approved of the New Deal was evident in Roosevelt's landslide reelection in 1936. In typical FDR fashion, he did not accept this victory as a cause for complacence. He faced the public squarely in his second inaugural address and he declared: "I see one-third of a nation ill-housed, ill-clad, ill-nourished." He acknowledged both the scope of the ongoing problems and the need to press on, energy unflagging, with reform, relief, and recovery.

FDR's second term proved more controversial than his first. A "court reform" plan he crafted and sponsored amounted to an attempt to pack the Supreme Court with judges favorable to many of his constitutionally questionable programs. In some places workers became increasingly militant—something for which FDR was blamed. When the Depression suddenly deepened in 1937, Roosevelt seemed uncharacteristically slow to respond with increased federal spending.

Despite these missteps both apparent and actual, national confidence in FDR himself remained largely unshaken. Nevertheless more conservatives were elected to Congress, which made it increasingly difficult for the president to promote his new programs.

On the menacing and ultimately cataclysmic international front during the Roosevelt presidency, FDR emphasized a very personal brand of diplomacy. Important FDR innovations in the

1930s included diplomatic recognition of the Soviet Union (still an outcast in much of the diplomatic community), the development of many reciprocal trade agreements, and the creation of a "good neighbor policy" toward the nations of Latin America. By the end of FDR's first term, it was clear that the militaristic dictatorships of Germany, Japan, and Italy boded ill for world peace, and Roosevelt's 1936 speech accepting renomination would prove prophetic: "This generation of Americans," he declared, "has a rendezvous with destiny."

Up to 1938 FDR, no isolationist, had reluctantly agreed to accept congressional neutrality acts designed to keep the United States out of another world war. By early 1939, however, the naked aggression of Germany compelled—or allowed—Roosevelt to take a much tougher position. He attempted to secure repeal of many of the provisions of the neutrality act, but did not succeed fully until November 1939, two months after World War II began in Europe with the Nazi invasion of Poland.

After gaining reelection to a third term in 1940, FDR initiated the lend-lease program to aid the anti-German allies. This innovative legislation provided an alternative to the cash-and-carry policy of supplying arms and matériel to Britain and other allies (including, as of June 1941, the U.S.S.R.), giving the president broad discretion to release war goods. FDR also authorized U.S. destroyers to escort convoys of Allied supply ships partway across the Atlantic. By December 1941 the United States and Germany were frankly engaged in an undeclared war on the Atlantic.

While focusing on German aggression, FDR also attempted to contain the aggressive expansion of Japan by imposing an embargo on the export of vital goods to that nation. Conceived as an alternative to war, this policy ultimately goaded Japanese militarists into attacking Pearl Harbor, Hawaii, on December 7, 1941, thereby propelling the United States into World War II.

As a wartime president, FDR took a hands-on approach to directing U.S. prosecution of the war, while promoting the rapid mobilization of industry at home. Among some African Americans at this time a semimilitant movement to end employment discrimination had begun. Seeking to avert racial disorder, Roosevelt set up a Fair Employment Practices Committee to prevent discrimination in defense-related employment—and thus he laid a cornerstone of the modern civil rights movement.

Contrary to what some of his conservative critics claimed, FDR was no socialist. He was quick to bring business leaders into policy-making positions, offering corporations generous contracts and tax breaks, and downgrading Progressive domestic reforms, all in the name of putting American industry on a war footing. This brought criticism from liberal supporters who felt themselves betrayed, but FDR, who had a clear vision of national priorities, was willing to make painful compromises.

The president's wartime leadership innovations included an emphasis on competition among advisers, industrialists, and others. Instead of appointing a single production czar to oversee the war effort, FDR harnessed pure capitalist principles, assuming that a competitive atmosphere would produce the best results. He did create a number of boards and agencies to control prices, develop manpower policy, and supervise the allocation of scarce materials. But for the most part, it was a zeal to win the war that fostered productive cooperation among workers, employers, and the government. FDR harnessed that zeal. By refusing to become a dictator, he transformed a war in defense of democracy under attack by totalitarianism into an all-out triumph of democratic methods and ideology.

Militarily Roosevelt accepted all responsibility and a great deal of criticism. Some condemned him for having left Pearl Harbor unprepared. Some even criticized him for cooperating with the "enemy," Vichy French admiral Jean Darlan, in planning the Allied invasion of North Africa. (By offering Darlan an opportunity to save face and preserve French honor, FDR avoided a full-scale armed confrontation with Vichy forces.) Others believed he was wrong to hold to a war policy that would accept nothing short of unconditional surrender. This, critics charged, discouraged anti-Hitler resistance within Germany. Even today most military thinkers believe Roosevelt was mistaken in his heavy reliance on strategic bombing in Europe, which never proved decisively effective, and many within the U.S. military community during the war believed FDR should have opened up the second front against Hitler earlier than the Normandy invasion (D-Day) of June 1944. But second guesses notwithstanding, FDR made all the necessary decisions, and what he decided ultimately resulted in victory by an alliance of very different nations—chiefly the United States, Britain, and the Soviet Union. Victory was achieved, and a difficult alliance held together.

Seeing victory in the offing, the people of the United States had sufficient confidence in FDR to elect him to a fourth term in 1944. If a third term was unprecedented, a fourth was even more remarkable. But it represented a tremendous sacrifice for the aging and ailing leader, whose health had deteriorated dramatically under the strains of war. FDR died early in his fourth term, on April 12, 1945, of a cerebral hemorrhage. He was only sixty-three.

Franklin Roosevelt is still regarded as one of the nation's most controversial leaders. Conservatives claimed and continue to claim that he transformed the federal government into a monster that destroyed states' rights and even compromised individual liberty. Many liberals criticized—and still criticize—him for taking insufficiently radical action against the Depression. On balance, however, historians consider Roosevelt one of America's great leaders, the greatest president of the twentieth century, and a shaper—almost certainly a savior—of modern America.

ON PURPOSE AND PRINCIPLE

SIMPLIFY AND MODERNIZE

"You cannot build a modern dynamo with the ancient forge and bellows of the medieval blacksmith."

—First gubernatorial inaugural address,
Albany, January 1, 1929

Like his early mentor and political hero, Woodrow Wilson, under whom he served as assistant secretary of the navy, Franklin Roosevelt was often accused of idealism during his long political career. Wilson responded to this accusation by admitting to the charge: "Sometimes people call me an idealist. Well, that is the way I know I am an American. America, my fellow citizens—I do not say it in disparagement of any other great people—America is the only idealistic nation in the world." In contrast to Wilson, FDR rarely responded in words but rather by action—that is, by finding the means to put ideals into actual operation. This would become the basis for the social policy of his two terms as New York governor and as president. Ideals were not so much discussed in a theoretical way as they were simply acted upon.

A key to Roosevelt's leadership was his genius for seamlessly joining idealism to practical action. For him the perfect piece of legislation, the perfect social program was one in which it was im-

3

possible to tell where theory stopped and practice started. They were one.

At the core of this genius was common sense, an understanding that ideals do not become actions by magic, but by mechanics—the mechanics of modern and efficient government. "You cannot build a modern dynamo with the ancient forge and bellows of the medieval blacksmith," he told his Albany audience in his first inaugural address as governor of New York. His point was that outmoded tools cannot produce products fit for the future. Government, the chief tool of social change, needed to be modernized not for the sake of modernity, but in order to become capable of creating policies and programs to carry into the future this enterprise called New York State.

To "take the first step toward . . . higher civilization," FDR declared, we "need to set our machinery of government in order . . . to simplify and modernize." For Roosevelt government was never an end, but a means to an end. It was an instrument, an implement for transforming ideals into action—a wonderful tool, but nothing more than that, and like any tool, its proper function was to be subordinate to the products it creates. The products in this case were social progress, social justice, an elevation of the common good, and the perfection of democracy. The simpler and more efficient a tool is, the better.

The less that comes between ideal and action, the better. Throughout his career FDR always focused on both modernizing and simplifying the mechanics of government so that government could become the extension of a collective will to transform the ideal into the real.

Poets have traditionally been regarded as the airiest sort of idealists, but the poets we have come to think of as most typically American—for example, Emily Dickinson and Walt Whitman in the nineteenth century and William Carlos Williams in the twentieth—focused very sharply on the commonplace, the everyday, the *real* reality. "No ideas," Williams once proclaimed, "no ideas but in things." And so we might think of Franklin Roosevelt as yet another typical American "poet," not only because of his drive to make the ideal and the real one and the same, but because of the way he expressed himself, communicated his message to the people he led. The British poet Percy Bysshe Shelley wrote: "Poets are the unacknowledged legislators of the world." Stand this on its head, and you have a description of Roosevelt at his eloquent best: the legislator as unacknowledged poet.

"You cannot build a modern dynamo with the ancient forge and bellows of the medieval blacksmith." Almost every word of this statement delivers an idea through a thing. The word "dynamo" conveys modernity, power, creativity, and the promise of the twentieth century, while "forge and bellows" evoke the past and, more important, the utter inadequacy of the past to the purpose of building the future.

"Simplify and modernize" is an important lesson for any leader to learn and learn right away. But perhaps an even more challenging lesson is implicit in this one. It is this: *A leader should be a poet.*

THAT IS OUR GOAL

*"That is our goal, and that goal will be understood by the
people of this country no matter where they live."*

—Speech to the 1932 Democratic National Convention,
Chicago, July 2, 1932

While it was happening, the Great Depression presented what appeared to be two starkly different images of suffering: on the one
hand, drought-stricken farmers standing helpless in the midst of a
Dust Bowl landscape; on the other, urban people, jobless, standing on bread lines. For many at the time, it seemed as if the one
image had little to do with the other, that the farmer's plight was
distinct from that of the industrial urban dweller. Persuading the
desperate city people to aid the farmer and the equally desperate
farmer to help those who lived in the city seemed an impossible
task. Yet FDR saw that it was essential to make the two halves of
the country, agricultural and industrial, see themselves as wholly
interdependent.

   "I know," FDR declared to the 1932 Democratic Convention,
"that every delegate in this hall who lives in the city knows why I
lay emphasis on the farmer. It is because one-half of our population, over fifty million people, are dependent on agriculture; and,
my friends, if those fifty million people have no money, no cash,

to buy what is produced in the city, the city suffers to an equal or greater extent."

From this analysis Roosevelt went on to do what all effective leaders do—establish a clear, worthwhile, and unambiguous goal:

> This is why we are going to make the voters understand this year that this nation is not merely a nation of independence, but it is, if we are to survive, bound to be a nation of interdependence—town and city, and North and South, East and West. That is our goal, and that goal will be understood by the people of this country no matter where they live.

It is not enough to state a goal. Whether or not that goal will be achieved depends in large part on *how* it is stated. FDR did not say "we should make the voters understand," but instead he declared far more positively "we are going to make the voters understand." An effective leader expresses what "we will" do rather than what "we should" do. Furthermore Roosevelt ensured that his audience understood that the goal he set is, in fact, "our" goal and he concluded by defining the word "our" in this context. "Our" takes in all "the people of this country no matter where they live." Politicians are accustomed to speaking of "our people" as a particular constituency: the people of Chicago, the people of Snellville, the farmers, the miners, the auto workers, and so on. Speaking directly to politicians, FDR set for them a goal that crossed all constituent boundaries, so that "our" encompassed all Americans.

A leader sets and articulates a goal; more important, she sets and articulates "our" goal. Just as she makes certain that the goal is understood unambiguously, she also ensures that the "our" includes everyone she leads.

SET PRIORITIES

"I favor as a practical policy the putting of first things first."

—First inaugural address, March 4, 1933

To those who called for improvement in international trade relations, FDR answered in his first inaugural address that this subject was indeed "vastly important," but "in point of time and necessity secondary to the establishment of a sound national economy. I favor as a practical policy the putting of first things first." He announced his intention to "spare no effort to restore world trade by international economic readjustment, but [he asserted even more strongly] the emergency at home cannot wait on that accomplishment."

It is one of a leader's most important responsibilities to sort out and establish priorities, to present these unambiguously, and then to act in accordance with them. Matters of immediate survival always take precedence over long-term issues, regardless of their apparent importance.

WHAT'S WORTH WINNING

"A selfish victory is always destined to be an ultimate defeat."

—Message to the nations of the world on disarmament,
May 16, 1933

In most transactions, whether among nations, businesses, or individuals, it is a destructive mistake to view success from the zero-sum point of view, the old idea that for every winner there must be a loser; for every gain on one side, there must be a loss on the other.

In most areas of human endeavor, business is conducted in a community. Value is exchanged for value. When this exchange fails, the result is little different from theft, the ultimate failure to exchange value for value. In a viable community of human endeavor, true victory is never selfish, but a triumph for all concerned.

This is not merely a statement of moral idealism. It is sound business and sound human policy. After all, how many selfish victories can you win before no one will trust you, no one will do business with you, no one will propose an exchange of value? A selfish victory, a one-sided "bargain," is necessarily a dead end, whereas a victory for all concerned, a transaction in which true value is exchanged for true value, necessarily leads to additional victories of this kind.

It is a mistake to focus exclusively on the short term, to be one of those storefront businesses that function under a permanent GOING OUT OF BUSINESS banner. Leading an enterprise into the future requires avoiding selfish victory and embracing exchanges in which all involved derive substantial benefit.

A RENDEZVOUS WITH DESTINY

"This generation of Americans has a rendezvous with destiny."
—Speech before the 1936 Democratic National Convention,
June 27, 1936

It has been a long time since we have dared to expect profound thought from our national leaders, and perhaps the very last place we look for profundity is at a political party convention. But in the magnificent, heartfelt speech FDR made before the 1936 convention of the Democratic Party, he expressed the core of his philosophy of leadership, a leadership based on "Charity—in the true spirit of that grand old word. For charity literally translated from the original means love." In that 1936 speech he also made an observation about his time and the people of his time that is profoundly inspiring:

> There is a mysterious cycle in human events. To some generations much is given. Of other generations much is expected. This generation of Americans has a rendezvous with destiny.

The great leaders, the courageous leaders, are not afraid to tell us who we are. Today few leaders in any context—business, gov-

11

ernment, or community—venture to make such assessments. And yet for time out of mind, it is to their leaders that people have looked for precisely such statements. A function of leadership is definition of the community, the organization, the enterprise—whatever one wishes to call the people a leader leads. In our leaders, we seek our identity. The great ones, the courageous leaders, do not disappoint us in that search.

THE GOAD OF FEAR AND SUFFERING

". . . our present gains were won under the pressure of more than ordinary circumstance. Advance became imperative under the goad of fear and suffering. The [hard] times were on the side of progress."

—Second inaugural address, January 20, 1937

Crisis and hard times, FDR well knew, are fraught with danger. In his first inaugural address, speaking to a nation at the nadir of economic desperation, the new president said that fear was the greatest enemy; that in fact we had "nothing to fear but fear itself." Once that fear had been faced, however, the nation moved with great energy through the introduction of radical new programs of aid and recovery. Under the "goad of fear and suffering," the "pressure of more than ordinary circumstance," Americans enthusiastically embraced the new initiatives.

Beginning his second term, Roosevelt was well aware that the Depression was still very much a fact of American life, but that fear and suffering had been reduced. This was a great and gratifying achievement, but FDR also understood that this achievement created a very real problem. Times of fear and suffering, he observed, "were on the side of progress":

To hold to progress today, however, is more difficult. Dulled conscience, irresponsibility, and ruthless self-interest already reappear. Such symptoms of prosperity may become portents of disaster! Prosperity already tests the persistence of our progressive purpose.

As difficult as it is to organize coherent and effective effort in times of pressing crisis, any competent leader is grateful for at least one feature of such times: motivation, the goad of fear and suffering. It takes more than merely competent leadership, however, to sustain coherent and effective effort after the crisis—or even the perception of crisis—has lifted. Absent the goad of an extraordinary situation, truly inspiring leadership is required to sustain the inspired action of the members of the enterprise. If fear is the first great obstacle a leader must overcome, surely complacency is the second.

Often Roosevelt's leadership task was to monitor and mirror progress, to demonstrate to the people that their collective situation had improved. He never painted a rosy picture but he did present the evidence of real progress. Acting as monitor and mirror in his second inaugural address, he now emphasized not how far the enterprise had come, but how much farther it had yet to travel. As usual for FDR, he engaged his audience. Like a skilled salesperson, he knew how to engage his prospects. This is not done by *telling* them what they should think, feel, or do, but by *asking* them questions that guide them on their own to the conclusions the salesperson wants them to reach.

> Let us ask again: Have we reached the goal of our vision of the fourth day of March 1933 [the occasion of the first inauguration]? Have we found our happy valley?

Unlike a salesperson, however, Roosevelt could not expect his inaugural audience to answer him. Instead he let the question

hang in the air and continued along another avenue of highly persuasive leadership communication. He still deliberately avoided
telling his audience anything. Instead he *showed* them. He delivered an eyewitness report, beginning with two powerful words:
"I see."

> I see a great nation, upon a great continent, blessed
> with a great wealth of natural resources. Its 130 million
> people are at peace among themselves; they are making
> their country a good neighbor among the nations. I see
> a United States which can demonstrate that, under
> democratic methods of government, national wealth
> can be translated into a spreading volume of human
> comfort hitherto unknown, and the lowest standard of
> living can be raised far above the level of mere subsis-
> tence.

Here is the potential of America, brightly rendered. Now comes
the contrast of current reality:

> But here is the challenge to our democracy: in this na-
> tion I see tens of millions of its citizens—a substantial
> part of its whole population—who at this very mo-
> ment are denied the greater part of what the very low-
> est standards of today call the necessities of life.

He continued with an eyewitness list of particulars:

> I see millions of families trying to live on incomes so
> meager that the pall of family disaster hangs over them
> day by day.
>   I see millions whose daily lives in city and on farm
> continue under conditions labeled indecent by a so-
> called polite society half a century ago.

> I see millions denied education, recreation, and the opportunity to better their lot and the lot of their children.
>
> I see millions lacking the means to buy the products of farm and factory and by their poverty denying work and productiveness to many other millions.
>
> I see one-third of a nation ill-housed, ill-clad, ill-nourished.

As monitor and mirror, a leader needs to present facts, personally, powerfully, persuasively. The more she lets the facts speak for themselves, without interpretation, the louder and clearer they speak.

Yet it would not be leadership merely to recite facts, no matter how eloquently. The effective leader presents the facts, lets them speak, then points the way through them:

> It is not in despair that I paint you that picture. I paint it for you in hope—because the nation, seeing and understanding the injustice in it, proposes to paint it out. We are determined to make every American citizen the subject of his country's interest and concern; and we will never regard any faithful, law-abiding group within our borders as superfluous.

Then he provides a sovereign standard for measuring the true progress of the nation and its democracy: "The test of our progress is not whether we add more to the abundance of those who have much; it is whether we provide enough for those who have too little."

Inspired leadership does not require the immediate agony of crisis. It does require a persuasive assessment of the current status of the enterprise, a crystal-clear picture of where we are *now*, added to a convincing assessment of our potential, where we *could* arrive, and a definite goal that reflects where we've been, where we are, and what we can reasonably expect to achieve. As for motive, an engine to drive the members of the enterprise together toward the desired goal, this cannot be furnished from outside. Inspired leadership presents the current situation together with the potential for improvement in such a way that those who are led draw their inspiration not directly from the leader, but from their own sense of justice, rightness, achievement, and excellence.

An inspired leader does not tell us what is best to do or think or believe but allows us to see the best for ourselves, and ultimately to act from motives of our own.

SACRED FIRE

"But if the spirit of America were killed, even though the nation's body and mind, constricted in an alien world, lived on, the America we know would have perished."

—Third inaugural address, January 20, 1941

Many leaders of organizations of all kinds—great corporations, small businesses, departments within larger firms, community groups, and so on—shy away from addressing the "spirit," the spirit within each individual and the collective spirit of the enterprise. Perhaps even more leaders do allow themselves to speak of spirit, but give it little specific definition or thought. For Franklin Roosevelt, however, a leader confronting some of the greatest challenges the United States ever faced, spirit was indeed the heart of the matter, and he gave it much thought and supremely eloquent expression.

There were those in America, understandably fearful of fighting a *second* world war, who advised negotiating with the dictators and attempting to live in isolation in a world dominated by totalitarianism. This might have preserved America physically—its mind and body—at least for a time, but constricted in such an "alien world," the "spirit of America" would die.

So what? Would that be so bad?

FDR explained the consequences of the death of the American spirit not in vague, abstract, or quasi-religious terms, but in words that evoke concepts and images all Americans cherish:

> That spirit—that faith—speaks to us in our daily lives in ways often unnoticed, because they seem so obvious. It speaks to us here in the capital of the nation. It speaks to us through the processes of governing in the sovereignties of forty-eight states. It speaks to us in our countries, in our cities, in our towns, and in our villages. It speaks to us from the other nations of the hemisphere, and from those across the sea—the enslaved, as well as the free. Sometimes we fail to hear or heed these voices of freedom because to us the privilege of our freedom is such an old, old story.
>
> The destiny of America was proclaimed in words of prophecy spoken by our first president in his first inaugural in 1789—words almost directed, it would seem, to this year of 1941: "The preservation of the sacred fire of liberty and the destiny of the republican model of government are justly considered . . . deeply, finally, staked on the experiment intrusted to the hands of the American people."
>
> If you and I in this later day lose that sacred fire—if we let it be smothered with doubt and fear—then we shall reject the destiny which Washington strove so valiantly and so triumphantly to establish. The preservation of the spirit and faith of the nation does, and will, furnish the highest justification for every sacrifice that we may make in the cause of national defense.

Every leader must create an understanding, for himself and for the group, of what constitutes the spirit of the enterprise. He must ask and answer just what it is that the enterprise cannot exist without. What element, if lost or changed, would destroy the essence of the organization? That element, whatever it may be, is the spirit of the organization—the one thing worth cherishing and defending at all cost. It is the sacred fire of the enterprise he leads.

LEADING TOWARD PERMANENCE

"The democratic aspiration is no mere recent phase in human history."

—Third inaugural address, January 20, 1941

An organization and its leader must be supple enough to antici-pate trends and challenges as they occur, yet at the core of this suppleness must be something rock hard and solid: a sense of en-during values and worthwhile principles. Few things are more damaging to an organization than leading it in pursuit of fads and will-o'-the-wisps. A grounding in solid values helps prevent this.

FDR reminded his inaugural day audience that at the core of the American enterprise is a "democratic aspiration" that is "no mere recent phase in human history. It is human history. It per-meated the ancient life of early peoples. It blazed anew in the Middle Ages. It was written in Magna Carta. . . . Its vitality was written into our own Mayflower Compact, into the Declaration of Independence, into the Constitution of the United States, into the Gettysburg Address."

FINDING A CAUSE

"It would be unworthy ... to exaggerate an isolated incident ..."

—Fireside Chat on national defense, September 11, 1941

History is littered with the folly of terrible wars triggered by comparatively trivial incidents deliberately magnified for the purpose of starting a war. It is all too easy to make highly consequential decisions on the basis of momentary emotion. On the other hand, history is also amply stocked with the disastrous consequences of failure to read the signs and respond to provocation. In presenting the case of the U.S. destroyer *Greer,* torpedoed by a German U-boat, Franklin Roosevelt took care to offer the incident not as an isolated occurrence—outrageous as it was—but as just one piece in the much larger Nazi pattern of heedless aggression: "piracy—piracy legally and morally. It was not the first nor the last act of piracy which the Nazi government has committed against the American flag in this war. For attack has followed attack." After detailing a series of incidents, FDR conceded: "It would be unworthy of a great nation to exaggerate an isolated incident, or to become inflamed by some one act of violence." And then he continued: "But it would be inexcusable folly to minimize such incidents in the face of evidence which makes it clear that the incident is not isolated, but is part of a general plan."

From this point on Roosevelt devoted the rest of the Fireside Chat to a careful exposition of Hitler's plan for "world mastery." He identified only one great obstacle still standing in the führer's way: the British navy.

> To be ultimately successful in world mastery, Hitler knows that he must get control of the seas. He must first destroy the bridge of ships which we are building across the Atlantic [to supply Britain] and over which we shall continue to roll the implements of war to help destroy him, to destroy all his works in the end. He must wipe out our patrol on sea and in the air if he is to do it. He must silence the British navy.
>
> I think it must be explained over and over again to people who like to think of the United States Navy as an invincible protection, that this can be true only if the British navy survives. And that, my friends, is simple arithmetic.

If "simple arithmetic" dictates continued United States support for the British war effort, FDR did not depend solely on emotionless numbers to make his case. He vividly etched the picture of Nazi tyranny:

> The Nazi danger to our Western world has long ceased to be a mere possibility. The danger is here now—not only from a military enemy but from an enemy of all law, all liberty, all morality, all religion.
>
> There has now come a time when you and I must see the cold, inexorable necessity of saying to these inhuman, unrestrained seekers of world conquest and

permanent world domination by the sword: "You seek to throw our children and our children's children into your form of terrorism and slavery. You have now attacked our own safety. You shall go no further." . . .

One peaceful nation after another has met disaster because each refused to look the Nazi danger squarely in the eye until it actually had them by the throat.

The United States will not make that fatal mistake.

Bear in mind that all of this powerful, persuasive rhetoric, this stirring call to and justification for action grows from FDR's interpretation of the attack on the *Greer*. Leadership is often about finding a cause and organizing action around it. The more concrete and specific the cause, the more successful group action is likely to be. To the degree that the endeavor is vague and abstract—or is stated in vague and abstract terms—the less successful the group's action is likely to be. An effective leader is able to focus group attention on a single meaningful reality. The leader draws conclusions and makes generalizations from this vividly realized reality. Action as well as principles flow from the reality he identifies. They are not vaguely and weakly applied to the situation *after* the fact. Action and principles that flow from concrete reality impress the group as absolutely necessary, justified, and urgent, whereas actions and principles vaguely arrived at carry the deadly taint of afterthought and rationalization. They invite doubt, and doubt invites failure.

THE GOAL BEYOND COMPROMISE

"I repeat that the United States can accept no result save victory, final and complete."

—Fireside Chat on war with Japan, December 9, 1941

One measure of our maturity—as adults, as members of a civilized society, as members of a family, and as businesspeople—is the willingness to compromise on a variety of issues day to day. This is a fact of life.

And yet a strong leader must define certain areas, certain goals, about which there can be no compromise. These constitute or reflect the core values of the organization she leads.

Whatever else Franklin Roosevelt was, he was a consummate politician. On this his admirers as well as his detractors agreed and still agree. Politics, we all know, is the art of compromise. But even this consummate politician knew when compromise was out of the question and he made it his business to ensure that the message of just what lay beyond compromise was always razor sharp:

> I repeat that the United States can accept no result save
> victory, final and complete. Not only must the shame
> of Japanese treachery be wiped out, but the sources of

international brutality, wherever they exist, must be absolutely and finally broken.

This was an incredibly bold statement, coming from the leader of a nation that had suffered total tactical defeat at Pearl Harbor and was rapidly losing ground in the Philippines and its other Pacific possessions. FDR demanded not just defense and survival, but victory: uncompromising triumph in the destruction, absolute and final, of "the sources of international brutality, wherever they exist."

In a situation as desperate as that of December 1941, how dare he set the bar of achievement so high?

What Roosevelt well appreciated is that it is precisely in the most desperate situations that one *must* set the bar the highest. The more desperate the threat, the greater the challenge, the more determined the effort must be and the more keen must be the understanding of just what values and goals lie beyond any question of compromise.

WHY WE FIGHT

"Together with all other free peoples, we are now fighting to maintain our right to live among our world neighbors in freedom and in common decency, without fear of assault."

—Fireside Chat on war with Japan, December 9, 1941

The corporate leader of twenty years ago and earlier was more or less a tyrant operating in a rigidly hierarchical organization. What he (and it was almost invariably *he*) said was law. Subordinates were just that, subordinates, from whom independent thought was neither required nor expected. Often it was actively discouraged. In such an organization the leader rarely felt obliged to explain, let alone justify, the course on which he led the organization. Everyone was expected to fall into line.

In most corporate organizations today, this approach to leadership is no longer acceptable—not because it makes people feel bad or seems unfair, but because most corporations have discovered what the champions of democratic government discovered more than two hundred years ago. Monolithic leadership, absolute monarchy, tyranny, whatever one calls it, is ineffective leadership. It sets up artificial barriers between the leader and the organization. It disenfranchises and demotivates the members of the organization. It deprives the enterprise of most of its energy, the energy of free people.

And so Roosevelt approached World War II, a war against tyrants and tyranny, as anything but a tyrannical leader. In the Fireside Chat he broadcast two days after the Pearl Harbor attack and one day after the United States' declaration of war on Japan, FDR offered the people a full explanation and justification of the course on which he was leading the nation.

He did not have to tell Americans that we were fighting because Pearl Harbor had been attacked. That much was obvious. He did not have to speak of self-defense or of revenge. These motives were obvious, too. Instead FDR proposed a nobler, more significant, and more enduring rationale for the fight: "Together with all other free peoples, we are now fighting to maintain our right to live among our world neighbors in freedom and in common decency, without fear of assault."

It is a stirring and urgent sentence. It presents a rationale of high and timeless purpose, but also one that is down to earth. It is neither abstract, nor overblown, nor difficult to grasp. It gives unity of purpose and direction to the titanic task ahead. Equally important, though, it is a rationale that enhances whatever individual reasons Americans may have had for fighting World War II. It does not replace those reasons. It does not declare them mistaken or misguided. It is compatible with simple self-defense as well as with an angry desire for vengeance.

A truly democratic leader, Roosevelt never told people what to think, much less what to feel. He provided inspiration and guidance for unified, coordinated action. He explained and justified the motives of government, but he never used such explanation and justification to "correct" the opinions or criticize the feelings of those he led.

Effective leadership harnesses the thought and the motivation of everyone. It guides rather than goads. It respects the individual, even as it leads individuals toward unified action. It appeals rather than compels.

KEEPING IT TOGETHER

"I want to make it clear that every American coal miner who has stopped mining coal—no matter how sincere his motives, no matter how legitimate he may believe his grievances to be— every idle miner directly and individually is obstructing our war effort. We have not yet won this war. We will win this war only as we produce and deliver our total American effort on the high seas and on the battlefronts. And that requires unrelenting, uninterrupted effort here on the home front."

—Fireside Chat on the federal seizure of the coal mines,
May 2, 1943

Leaders must never make the mistake of believing that they lead a company, a department, or a unit. What they lead are the individuals who make up that enterprise. It is all too easy to think of an organization as a monolith, a single, solid thing that can be pointed unerringly in a particular direction. In fact such a group is a collection of people, each of whom is subject to distraction and each of whom may, for a variety of reasons, begin to follow a separate agenda.

In organizing and, even more important, in sustaining any extended, complex enterprise, it becomes crucial to maintain focus without neglecting or alienating any of the individuals who make up the group. Providing motivation consists in part of generating enthusiasm, energy, and determination to achieve a certain objective, but it also requires guiding people away from misspending their enthusiasm, energy, and determination on individual issues that do not contribute to the common goal.

Fully grasping that he was leader of a democratic society, Franklin Roosevelt, shortly after Pearl Harbor, met with the three great labor organizations of the time: the American Federation of Labor (AFL), the Congress of Industrial Organizations (CIO), and the Railroad Brotherhoods. All agreed that there would be no strikes as long as the war lasted. The United Mine Workers subsequently signed on to that pledge, but requested that a War Labor Board be established to settle any disputes that could not be resolved through collective bargaining.

In the spring of 1943 a dispute erupted between the coal miners and the coal companies. The War Labor Board was called in, but all efforts at conciliation and mediation failed. A general strike was called, and in response President Roosevelt ordered the government to take control of the mines. The day after this order was issued, FDR addressed the nation in one of his Fireside Chats.

The mining crisis was twofold. First, as FDR explained, "stopping . . . the coal supply, even for a short time, would involve a gamble with the lives of American soldiers and sailors and the future security of our whole people. It would involve an unwarranted, unnecessary, and terribly dangerous gamble with our chances for victory." Second, however, in a democracy, any seizure of private industry and intervention in labor disputes threatened basic rights and values. The potential for alienating a large segment of the nation was very real. Thus FDR was presented with a classic leadership problem: Resolve one crisis without creating another and maintain focus on collective goals without alienating individuals whose work is essential to achieving those goals.

The president sought resolution, first, by making an effort to maintain for the immediate present progress toward the organization's principal goal. He seized the coal mines to ensure that the war effort would proceed without interruption. Only after he had taken this action did he work to avert the secondary crisis that would result from miner alienation. This action was a public appeal to the miners in the form of a Fireside Chat.

He did not scold or accuse. Indeed he acknowledged the sincerity of the miners' cause and beliefs. But he appealed to values transcending that cause and those beliefs: "Tonight, I am speaking to the essential patriotism of the miners, and to the patriotism of their wives and children." After recounting the events of the past few days in an effort to show that the decision to strike was "arbitrary," FDR shifted from the important and value-loaded abstraction of "patriotism" to something immediately ("this split second") real to the miners:

> You miners have sons in the army and navy and Marine Corps. You have sons who at this very minute—this split second—may be fighting in New Guinea, or in the Aleutian Islands, or Guadalcanal, or Tunisia, or China, or protecting troop ships and supplies against submarines on the high seas. We have already received telegrams from some of our fighting men overseas, and I only wish they could tell you what they think of the stoppage of work in the coal mines.
>
> Some of your own sons have come back from the fighting fronts, wounded. A number of them, for example, are now here in an army hospital in Washington. Several of them have been decorated by their government.
>
> I could tell you of one from Pennsylvania. He was a coal miner before his induction, and his father is a coal miner. He was seriously wounded by Nazi machine-gun bullets while he was on a bombing mission over Europe in a Flying Fortress.

Another boy, from Kentucky, the son of a coal miner, was wounded when our troops first landed in North Africa six months ago.

There is still another, from Illinois. He was a coal miner—his father and two brothers are coal miners. He was seriously wounded in Tunisia while attempting to rescue two comrades whose jeep had been blown up by a Nazi mine.

These men do not consider themselves heroes. They would probably be embarrassed if I mentioned their names over the air. They were wounded in the line of duty. They know how essential it is to the tens of thousands—hundreds of thousands and ultimately millions of other young Americans to get the best of arms and equipment into the hands of our fighting forces, and get them there quickly. The fathers and mothers of our fighting men, their brothers and sisters and friends—and that includes all of us—are also in the line of duty: the production line. Any failure in production may well result in costly defeat on the field of battle.

To create and maintain the focus, a leader must use words to get beyond words, to get to facts and to feelings. And this FDR did by making the goals of the nation immediately relevant and real to the striking miners. He demonstrated—not by telling, but by showing—that the nation's goals *are* those of the miners themselves. He then went on to acknowledge just how heavily invested in those goals the miners truly are. Not only was uninterrupted progress toward national purposes essential to the well-being of the miners' fighting sons, to prevent *their* efforts and sacrifices from having been made in vain, it was also consistent with the miners' own efforts and sacrifices:

There can be no one among us—no one faction—powerful enough to interrupt the forward march of our people to victory. You miners have ample reason to know that there are certain basic rights for which this country stands, and that those rights are worth fighting for and worth dying for. That is why you have sent your sons and brothers from every mining town in the nation to join in the great struggle overseas. That is why you have contributed so generously, so willingly, to the purchase of war bonds and to the many funds for the relief of war victims in foreign lands. That is why, since this war was started in 1939, you have increased the annual production of coal by almost two hundred million tons a year.

The greatest obstacle any motivator must overcome is inertia. Inertia is the physical law that tends to keep a motionless body motionless. But there is more to the law of inertia than motionlessness. Once a body is in motion, inertia tends to keep it in motion, at the same velocity, and in the same direction. A skilled motivator, FDR sought to exploit here this second property of inertia, by reminding the miners that they were already in motion, already committed, deeply committed, to the war effort. Thus FDR's task was not to get them moving, but to keep them moving, to guide them in maintaining their demonstrated commitment, to persuade them to protect the heavy investment they have already made, personally and individually, in the war effort. He went on to render the reality of this commitment not just in intellectual terms, but in a visceral dimension as well:

The toughness of your sons in our armed forces is not surprising. They come of fine, rugged stock. Men who work in the mines are not unaccustomed to hardship.

And then, with great rhetorical skill, Roosevelt used the subject of hardship to acknowledge the legitimacy of the miners' concerns and grievances and to assure the miners that the government was committed to addressing them:

> It has been the objective of this government to reduce that hardship, to obtain for miners and for all who do the nation's work a better standard of living.
>
> I know only too well that the cost of living is troubling the miners' families, and troubling the families of millions of other workers throughout the country as well.
>
> A year ago it became evident to all of us that something had to be done about living costs. Your government determined not to let the cost of living continue to go up as it did in the First World War.

The president went on to detail the price controls that were and would be put into place. Having done this, however, he returned to the central theme of his Fireside Chat: "The war is going to go on. Coal will be mined no matter what any individual thinks about it. . . . And so, under these circumstances, it is inconceivable that any patriotic miner can choose any course other than going back to work and mining coal." Even here, however, the operative verb was *choose*.

Federal seizure of the coal mines was a forceful step, but in the final analysis, Roosevelt understood what all successful leaders understand. Force and coercion are sometimes necessary, but they only carry so far. No truly sustainable enterprise can be led by force and coercion, not over the long term. Ultimately, an enterprise is sustained by the remarkable coincidence of self-interest and selfless commitment to collective values. A leader's task is to make each member of the organization aware of this link between self and group, so that each individual is in a position to *choose* a course beyond immediate self-interest. A leader ignites motivation, but the fire that drives each individual toward common goals is a fire that burns within.

FDR concluded not on a threatening note of coercion, but of moral suasion: "Tomorrow, the Stars and Stripes will fly over the coal mines, and I hope that every miner will be at work under that flag."

LOOK BEYOND CRISIS

"A sound postwar economy is a major present responsibility."

—Statement on signing the G.I. Bill of Rights,
June 22, 1944

Little more than two weeks after the Allies landed on the beaches of Normandy in the greatest and riskiest military invasion in history, at a point in time when the nation's mind, heart, and muscle were focused on the tremendous effort of the present, Franklin Roosevelt looked to the future. He signed into law the G.I. Bill of Rights, a series of economic and other benefits designed to reintegrate millions of returning veterans into civilian society. Thanks to this legislation, millions of young Americans would in fact *begin* their civilian careers with technical training, with a college education, and with business and agricultural loans.

A great crisis or all-consuming project demands full-time attention and effort, and yet it is a mistake to lead only for the crisis or the project at hand. A great enterprise requires continuity. Even in the midst of an all-consuming task, leadership of such an enterprise calls for acknowledgment of the future, in part to demonstrate faith in the future and in part to avert some new crisis in the times ahead. The sentence with which FDR concluded his statement on signing the G.I. Bill of Rights should serve as a reminder to all leaders, no matter how deeply buried they and their organizations may be in the immediate challenges of the on-going "war" that is the hurly-burly of the here and now: "A sound postwar economy is a major present responsibility." Whatever the demands of the present, do not forsake the future.

EYES ON THE PRIZE

". . . victory is not . . . an end in itself . . ."

—Message to Congress urging adoption of the Bretton
Woods agreements, February 12, 1945

In July 1944, at a conference in Bretton Woods, New Hampshire, the United States signed an international agreement to establish fixed monetary exchange rates, to create an International Monetary Fund, and, of most urgent importance, to found an International Bank for Reconstruction and Development. The Bretton Woods agreements did nothing less than create the framework for a stable postwar economic system and, in this way, were a cornerstone of the United Nations and other postwar international organizations. Signed in 1944, the key measures came up for Congressional approval the following year.

President Roosevelt was anxious to ensure that the United States did not make the same shortsighted mistakes it had made after World War I. President Woodrow Wilson had taken a leading role in crafting the League of Nations, an international forum aimed at preventing future war, only to endure the bitter and tragic disappointment of Congressional rejection of the League. Without United States support, the League of Nations proved ineffectual, and two decades after the "war to end all wars" had ended, a *second* world war began. FDR was determined not to win this second war only, for a second time, to lose the peace that followed it.

He faced a problem many leaders of major projects face: maintaining momentum toward the *final* goal. It is all too easy to mistake objectives for goals. Objectives are the milestones that must be attained in order to reach the ultimate marker, the goal. Often great and complex undertakings involve many objectives and many milestones. It is the leader's task to urge the organization from one objective to the next and to acknowledge and celebrate the attainment of each. But it is also the leader's task to keep the eyes of the enterprise focused on the final prize:

> As we dedicate our total efforts to the task of winning this war we must never lose sight of the fact that victory is not only an end in itself but, in a large sense, victory offers us the means of achieving the goal of lasting peace and a better way of life. Victory does not insure the achievement of these larger goals; it merely offers us the opportunity—the chance—to seek their attainment. Whether we will have the courage and vision to avail ourselves of this tremendous opportunity—purchased at so great a cost—is yet to be determined. On our shoulders rests the heavy responsibility for making this momentous decision. I have said before, and I repeat again: This generation has a rendezvous with destiny.
>
> If we are to measure up to the task of peace with the same stature as we have measured up to the task of war, we must see that the institutions of peace rest firmly on the solid foundations of international political and economic cooperation.

The president continued with a concise outline of the United States' role in international reconstruction and redevelopment and of the nation's sponsorship role in creating a United Nations, a true world forum and alternative to war.

> The point in history at which we stand is full of promise and of danger. The world will either move toward unity and widely shared prosperity or it will move apart into necessarily competitive economic blocs. We have a chance, we citizens of the United States, to use our influence in favor of a more united and cooperating world. Whether we do so will determine, as far as it is in our power, the kind of lives our grandchildren can live.

THEME TWO

ON HARD FACT AND HARD RESPONSIBILITY

REFUSE TO BECOME
DESTINY'S PRISONER

"I refuse to believe that the world is, of necessity, such a prisoner of destiny."

—Message to Chancellor Adolf Hitler and
Premier Benito Mussolini, April 14, 1939

By early 1939 it was clear to all but those who willfully refused to see that Germany's Adolf Hitler and Italy's Benito Mussolini were bent on aggressive conquest. Most immediately, it was apparent that Hitler, having annexed Austria and gobbled up Czechoslovakia, had his sights set on Poland. In September of 1938 at Munich, British prime minister Neville Chamberlain, naively pursuing his policy of "active appeasement" of Hitler's ambitions, sold out Czechoslovak sovereignty in exchange for the führer's assurance that he had no more designs for expansion. Chamberlain returned from the Munich Conference and, from the front door of 10 Downing Street, waved the piece of paper signed by "Herr Hitler." "My good friends, this is the second time in our history that there has come back from Germany to Downing Street peace with honor. I believe it is peace for our time. I thank you from the bottom of our hearts. And now I recommend you go home and sleep quietly in your beds."

FDR understood that the world—the free world, the world of

democratic nations—had been sleeping for too long and he also understood that soon few in any part of the world would be sleeping quietly. On the eve of what seemed the certainty of war, Roosevelt sent a public message to Hitler and Mussolini, not warning them of retaliation, but appealing to them not to surrender their decency and free will by capitulating to a concept of "destiny," which for them meant the inevitability of war and conquest.

> . . . the tide of events seems to have reverted to the threat of arms. If such threats continue, it seems inevitable that much of the world must become involved in common ruin. All the world—victor nations, vanquished nations, and neutral nations—will suffer. I refuse to believe that the world is, of necessity, such a prisoner of destiny. On the contrary, it is clear that the leaders of great nations have it in their power to liberate their peoples from the disaster that impends.

In hindsight Roosevelt's attempt to awaken Hitler and Mussolini to their responsibility as leaders of great nations seems a hopeless appeal. It was an appeal to decency, and the two dictators were manifestly indecent people.

Yet FDR's leadership message outlives April 1939, remains important, and is, in fact, timeless. A leader's failure to come to terms with the reality of a particular time, place, and situation can have catastrophic results—as Neville Chamberlain and the world would learn all too bitterly. But it is important to understand that acknowledging and coming to grips with reality is not the same as surrendering to destiny. Destiny, by definition, cannot be altered. To yield to destiny is to abandon leadership. Reality, however, can be shaped, directed, even radically changed—provided that reality is first acknowledged, understood, and confronted. These three functions—acknowledging, understanding, and confronting things as they are—are the first stages of any effective leadership act.

MANAGE INFORMATION

"Do not believe of necessity everything you hear or read. Check up on it first."

—Fireside Chat on the war in Europe, September 3, 1939

At four-thirty on the morning of September 1, 1939, without declaration of any kind, the Luftwaffe (air force) of Adolf Hitler's Germany bombed airfields all across Poland. Simultaneously, a German battleship "visiting" the Polish port of Danzig (Gdansk) opened fire on Polish fortifications, and the German Wehrmacht (army) surged in massive numbers across the Polish frontier. World War II had begun in Europe.

On September 3 Franklin Roosevelt made the war in Europe the subject of a Fireside Chat. His primary message was a wake-up call for America, a warning that, while we were an ocean away from the battlefield, the war would surely touch us: "Passionately though we may desire detachment, we are forced to realize that every word that comes through the air, every ship that sails the sea, every battle that is fought does affect the American future."

FDR prepared the nation for the day he knew all too well would come: the day of America's entry into a new world war.

Before he delivered that message, however, FDR was anxious

to manage information. Anyone who has ever led or managed an organization consisting of more than two people knows the power and persistence of rumor. The office grapevine can be a remarkably useful source of information but it is also a heedless producer of misinformation, distorted and partial facts, and even malicious falsehood. A leader needs to manage information—to get a firm hand on the rumor mill—yet to do so without giving the impression of censorship and concealment and without *telling* people what to think. Clumsy, heavy-handed management of information will not suppress rumor, but will only serve to intensify it, even as it creates distrust of leadership. No leader can afford to allow the members of the enterprise to believe that their leader is withholding important facts, distorting them, "spinning" them, or out-and-out lying about them.

FDR understood this and in this Fireside Chat he wisely approached the issue of information management by transferring part of the burden from the government to the people:

> You are, I believe, the most enlightened and the best informed people in all the world at this moment. You are subjected to no censorship of news, and I want to add that your government has no information which it withholds or which it has any thought of withholding from you.
>
> At the same time, as I told my press conference on Friday, it is of the highest importance that the press and the radio use the utmost caution to discriminate between actual verified fact on the one hand, and mere rumor on the other.
>
> I can add to that by saying that I hope the people of this country will also discriminate most carefully between news and rumor. Do not believe of necessity everything you hear or read. Check up on it first.

The most effective leaders avoid pushing or pulling those they lead. Instead they persuade, they guide, they direct, and they motivate. It is neither possible nor desirable for a leader to control everything members of the organization hear or say, but it is crucially important that the leader clearly charges everyone with the responsibility of managing information by discriminating between fact and rumor. As a particular project or situation progresses, leadership must communicate as freely and as reliably as security and other considerations permit. At the same time, it is the leader's responsibility to monitor communication within the organization and to address any rumors or misinformation that surface—all the while reminding the members of the organization that information management is key to success and that ultimately, it begins and ends with each of them.

FACE THE COLD, HARD FACTS

"What we face is cold, hard fact."

—Radio address announcing an unlimited
national emergency, May 27, 1941

Recognizing that the design for Hitler's "new world order" would not stop with the conquest of Europe, President Roosevelt worked vigorously with the other nations of the hemisphere— the Latin American members of the Pan-American Union and Canada—to unite in military and political alliance all of the American republics against Nazi and other aggression. To free up his executive power to order rapid troop mobilization, to accelerate the build-up of military forces, and to step up war production, FDR also declared an "unlimited national emergency." He explained this step in a radio address.

No crisis is overcome through panic, but neither can it be coped with by ignorance either willful or unintended. A leader faces facts and guides the entire organization in facing them as well.

The pressing problems that confront us are military and naval problems. We cannot afford to approach

them from the point of view of wishful thinkers or sen-
timentalists. What we face is cold, hard fact.

The first and fundamental fact is that what started
as a European war has developed, as the Nazis always
intended it should develop, into a world war for world
domination.

Adolf Hitler never considered domination of Europe as an end in itself. European conquest was but a
step toward ultimate goals in all the other continents.
It is unmistakably apparent to all of us that, unless the
advance of Hitlerism is forcibly checked now, the
Western Hemisphere will be within range of the Nazi
weapons of destruction.

Here is a forceful but not panicky statement of fact. There is
no hedging—this *could* happen or that *might* occur. Rather, it is a
statement governed by verbs indicating accomplished fact—*is,
was, has developed*—and by a simple future tense: *will be.* Of
course, there is another vital word in this statement: *unless.*

A leader should not only be able to face facts squarely and
communicate them clearly, but also be able to analyze and present
the consequences of those facts, using the straightforward terms
of causal expression: *if, then, unless.* There is no clearer or more
forceful way of understanding a situation, expressing that situation, and presenting the range of actions available.

LOOK AT THE RECORD

"I have prepared the full record . . ."

—Fireside Chat on war with Japan, December 9, 1941

A leader has no asset more valuable and no tool more effective than the truth. It is important, then, to tell the truth, but it is even more important to allow those you lead to see and recognize the truth for themselves.

How do you do this?

Look at the record.

In explaining to the American people the war against Japan, President Roosevelt opened the record by presenting it in a straightforward, even bare-bones style:

> The course that Japan has followed for the past ten years in Asia has paralleled the course of Hitler and Mussolini in Europe and in Africa. Today, it has become far more than a parallel. It is actual collaboration so well calculated that all the continents of the world, and all the oceans, are now considered by the Axis strategists as one gigantic battlefield.
>
> In 1931, ten years ago, Japan invaded Manchukuo [Manchuria]—without warning.

In 1935, Italy invaded Ethiopia—without warning.

In 1938, Hitler occupied Austria—without warning.

In 1939, Hitler invaded Czechoslovakia—without warning.

Later in 1939, Hitler invaded Poland—without warning.

In 1940, Hitler invaded Norway, Denmark, the Netherlands, Belgium, and Luxembourg—without warning.

In 1940, Italy attacked France and later Greece—without warning.

And this year, in 1941, the Axis powers attacked Yugoslavia and Greece and they dominated the Balkans—without warning.

In 1941, also, Hitler invaded Russia—without warning.

And now Japan has attacked Malaya and Thailand—and the United States—without warning.

It is all of one pattern.

Who says lists are boring? If the information is compelling, a simple, forcefully presented list is a dramatic and persuasive method of bringing truth to the people or rather, bringing people to the truth. Whenever possible turn to the record and allow it to speak for you.

KILL RUMORS

". . . pass from the realm of rumor and poison to the field of facts . . ."

—Fireside Chat on the war, February 23, 1942

Never underestimate the destructive force of a rumor. Few things erode morale, confidence, focus, and determination faster or more thoroughly. Do not ignore rumors. Catch them and counter them with reliable facts even if those facts are hard to take. The truth is always preferable to rumor, as fact is always preferable to fantasy:

> To pass from the realm of rumor and poison to the field of facts: the number of our officers and men killed in the attack on Pearl Harbor on December seventh was 2,340, and the number wounded was 940. Of all of the combatant ships based on Pearl Harbor—battleships, heavy cruisers, light cruisers, aircraft carriers, destroyers and submarines—only three were permanently put out of commission.
>
> Very many of the ships of the Pacific Fleet were not even in Pearl Harbor. Some of those that were there were hit very slightly, and others that were damaged

have either rejoined the Fleet by now or are still undergoing repairs. And when those repairs are completed, the ships will be more efficient fighting machines than they were before.

The report that we lost more than a thousand planes at Pearl Harbor is as baseless as the other weird rumors. The Japanese do not know just how many planes they destroyed that day, and I am not going to tell them. But I can say that to date—and including Pearl Harbor—we have destroyed considerably more Japanese planes than they have destroyed of ours.

THEME THREE

ON CREDIBILITY

SPEAK THE TRUTH

"This is preeminently the time to speak the truth, the whole truth, frankly and boldly."

—First inaugural address, March 4, 1933

One of Franklin Roosevelt's greatest speeches was his first inaugural address, the most memorable line of which is still familiar to the majority of Americans: "The only thing we have to fear is fear itself." But before FDR took us to that line, he began, as many effective leaders do, by making a contract with those he leads: "I am certain that my fellow Americans expect that on my induction into the presidency I will address them with a candor and a decision which the present situation of our nation impels." In this statement the new president articulated his understanding of what the American people wanted and expected from him: candor and decision. This statement is a contract in the truest sense—not a one-way but a two-way mutual agreement. For FDR's declaration of his certainty that Americans wanted candor and decision from him implied his understanding that the American people were willing to *hear* and *heed* that candor and decision; that they were willing to face the truth.

Contracts are intended to prevent dispute and disappointment. They are different from promises. A promise is a one-way agreement: This is what I shall give you. A contract, however, is a bargain, an exchange of value in return for value. As a leader FDR rarely made promises but he often made contracts—pledging something in return for something. The greatest single message of his leadership was that the democratic enterprise can never be passive. All must contribute, sacrifice, and endure, all must give of their value to obtain the value of democracy. This is the contract of America.

GET REAL

"I do not promise that every bank will be reopened or that in-dividual losses will not be suffered, but there will be no losses that possibly could be avoided; and there would have been more and greater losses had we continued to drift."

—Fireside Chat on the banking crisis, March 12, 1933

Franklin Roosevelt was justly celebrated for his contagious opti-mism. Anyone who has seen newsreel footage of FDR speaking is struck by his smile and his positive, confident, even buoyant body language—despite his being a paraplegic. His words, too, always conveyed hope. Yet charisma and sunny words would soon have seemed hollow mockery without the presence of a core of reality to justify the optimism. FDR never missed an opportunity to put the truth in the best *possible* light, but he never indulged in sub-stanceless fantasy. He knew that to do this would quickly destroy the confidence people had in his leadership, in the entire govern-ment, and, most of all, in themselves.

In his Fireside Chat on the banking crisis, he gave it to his au-dience straight, the good news with the bad, confident that the good news outweighed the bad. He counted on the people's abil-ity to weigh for themselves what he had to say. He did not rely on their willingness to believe in miracles he could not create.

STAND ON YOUR RECORD

"My record as governor and as president proves my devotion to [civil and religious] liberties. You who know me can have no fear that I would tolerate the destruction by any branch of government of any part of our heritage of freedom."

—Fireside Chat on reorganization of the judiciary, March 9, 1937

Franklin Roosevelt's attempt to pack the Supreme Court with justices likely to favor his policies (see "Lesson Learned," pages 231–33) brought charges from some quarters that he was threatening basic rights guaranteed by the Constitution. FDR sought to counter this accusation with an appeal to his record and his personal integrity. Both of these—a record of ethical achievement and a reputation for unimpeachable integrity—are coin of the realm for any leader. It is always best to bolster your policies and positions by resorting to the present facts of the present issue; however, there may well come a time when a leader must make an appeal to personal confidence. As long as the leader's record of high character and integrity is sound, such a plea is a very effective leadership tool. Allow an erosion of ethics, however, and the appeal will have an effect precisely opposite of what is intended.

ASSERT CREDIBILITY

". . . I tell you the blunt fact . . ."

—Fireside Chat on national defense, September 11, 1941

By mid 1941 the United States, a neutral nation in World War II, was in fact conducting an undeclared naval war in the North Atlantic. United States warships escorted convoys between the U.S. mainland and Greenland and on several occasions engaged German U-boats in combat.

In a Fireside Chat on September 11, 1941, FDR reported to the American people that the U.S.S. *Greer,* a destroyer, had been torpedoed by a U-boat while delivering mail to Greenland military outposts. Here was an outright act of war against a U.S. ship—one of several such acts during this period—and yet, as FDR was well aware, there were many in America who would refuse to accept it as an act of war and instead would willfully close their eyes to all that the aggression implied.

Roosevelt faced problems many leaders must contend with: How do you assert your credibility? How do you cut through rumor, propaganda, illusion, and self-delusion? How do you make your point of view count more strongly than any other?

FDR asserted his claim to credibility by forceful language, a willingness to lay his reputation 100 percent on the line: "In spite of what Hitler's propaganda bureau has invented, and in spite of what any American obstructionist organization may prefer to believe, I tell you the blunt fact that the German submarine fired first upon this American destroyer without warning, and with deliberate design to sink her."

Persuading others that what you have to say is the truth, the whole truth, and nothing but the truth is certainly easier if you have the facts—the evidence—to back your assertions. In the course of this Fireside Chat, FDR did present the evidence. Yet it is crucially important for a leader to recognize that he is not in a court of law. In such a court the evidence is paramount because all people, great or small, are equal in the eyes of the law. In the court of public opinion, however, which is the venue of all leaders, personal character, reputation, and record take precedence over evidence. FDR traded on these to deliver an extraordinarily forceful leadership statement. His message was this: *It is true because I tell you it is true.*

This is the place at which any effective leader must somehow arrive, a position of total credibility, a position from which a forceful, lay-it-on-the-line statement of blunt fact is taken without question as a statement of just that: blunt fact.

Any leader who wishes to gauge his credibility should ponder this sentence: "In spite of what Hitler's propaganda bureau has invented, and in spite of what any American obstructionist organization may prefer to believe, I tell you the blunt fact that the German submarine fired first upon this American destroyer without warning, and with deliberate design to sink her."

Now ask yourself: Could I say the equivalent—"Despite what you have heard, this is the fact"—and be believed? The only meaningful answer to this question is "yes" or "no." And that answer is the unerring gauge of your present ability to lead whatever organization is in your charge.

KEEP YOUR WORD

"We promised to return; we have returned."

—Statement on the landing of U.S. troops
in the Philippines, October 20, 1944

December 7, 1941, was certainly not the last dark day for America in World War II. Immediately after the attack on Pearl Harbor, other U.S. possessions in the Pacific fell under attack, including the Philippines. After a gallant defense, U.S. and Filipino forces commanded by Lieutenant General Jonathan Wainwright surrendered to the Japanese on May 6, 1942. Wainwright's commander, Douglas MacArthur, had been ordered by President Roosevelt to evacuate to Australia. He did so on March 11, 1942, and once he reached safety on March 17, he broadcast to the Philippines and the world perhaps the most famous promise any military commander has ever made: "I shall return."

For most who heard that promise in 1942, it must have seemed at best no more than an expression of hope and, at worst, empty words. Then, in October 1944, with the U.S. invasion of the Philippines under way, President Roosevelt took the opportunity to point out that the promise was being kept.

A leader must husband his credibility. His word is coin of the realm. Its value must be rigorously upheld. Allow it to become debased, and very little afterward can be accomplished. Keep your promises and make certain the keeping of them is universally known, understood, and appreciated.

THEME FOUR

ON MAKING CONTACT

ALL POLICY IS HUMAN POLICY

"The essential qualities of a true Pan-Americanism must be the same as those which constitute a good neighbor, namely, mutual understanding, and, through such understanding, a sympathetic appreciation of the other's point of view."

—Address to the governing board of the
Pan-American Union, April 12, 1933

The single most important item of foreign policy in Roosevelt's first term as president was the creation of a Good Neighbor Policy with the nations of Latin America. It was a policy intended to bring political, diplomatic, and economic unity and stability to our hemisphere by redressing the all too legitimate grievances some Latin American nations had against the United States. Since at least the era of the Spanish-American War near the end of the nineteenth century, many Americans tended to treat the Latin American states as unofficial vassals or client countries. The result was disunity within the hemisphere and, in many cases, outright anti-U.S. sentiment.

"Foreign policy" is a lofty phrase, and diplomats are accustomed to conducting their business on a lofty plane, but FDR, characteristically, brought policy down to earth. He chose the phrase *good neighbor* because everyone in the United States and in the other nations of the hemisphere would understand it. He took pains to show that his idea of friendship and cooperation among nations was less a political concept than, quite simply, a human one. Pan-Americanism, another high-sounding concept, he stated, was precisely the same as being a good neighbor.

Expressing foreign policy in human terms was not a way to "dumb down" diplomacy for the man and woman in the street, although it certainly did help to make such policy more meaningful to ordinary people. No mere simplification, it was instead an expression of the ultimately human basis of all policy, no matter how complex. Relations among nations are relations among people. FDR understood this, just as any effective business manager understands that relations between companies are really people relations. Diplomacy is a people business, and business is a people business. Shallow commentators might dismiss the concept of a good neighbor policy as a fiction or a metaphor to represent the far more complex reality of an international policy. In truth it is abstractions such as the very phrase "international policy" that are the fictions. The *reality* always comes down to people and the relations between and among them. No truly effective leader ever allows an abstraction to get between her and those with whom she works.

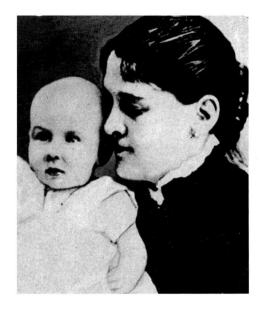

Sara Delano Roosevelt with her infant son Franklin, 1882.

Young Master Franklin dressed for riding.

Franklin Delano Roosevelt, child of wealth and privilege, about 1886.

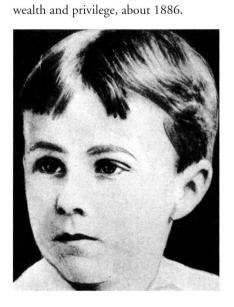

All images from ArtToday except where noted.

Front and center with his second-squad teammates on the Groton School football team, about 1898.

With his father, James, and mother, Sara Delano, May 1899. James Roosevelt died in 1900; this was the last family portrait.

Eleanor Roosevelt, niece of Theodore Roosevelt, distant cousin—and bride—of Franklin Roosevelt, on her wedding day, March 17, 1905.

FDR's debut on the national scene, as assistant secretary of the Navy under Josephus Daniels in the cabinet of President Woodrow Wilson. He served from 1913 to 1920.

FDR was nominated as the Democratic Party's vice presidential candidate and running mate to James M. Cox (*left*) in 1920. Here the pair doff their boaters on the campaign trail. *(Image from the Library of Congress.)*

In 1921, FDR was stricken with polio and lost the use of his legs. Swimming and bathing, especially in the natural warm springs of Warm Springs, Georgia, became Roosevelt's chief lifelong means of physical therapy. Here he is pictured at Warm Springs in the 1930s.

Harry Hopkins, Roosevelt's closest confidant (except for wife Eleanor), headed the WPA during the Depression and was the president's chief adviser during World War II. He is shown here with his daughter and the president.

No American president—no world leader—had a more infectious smile. President/candidate Roosevelt is pictured here in 1940. *(Image from the National Archives and Records Administration.)*

Roosevelt campaigns for an unprecedented third term in the White House. His motorcade drives by the headquarters of his opponent, Wendell Willkie, 1940.

(Image from the National Archives and Records Administration.)

Girding for war in 1940, FDR initiated the first and largest U.S. peacetime draft in history. The president looks on as a blindfolded Secretary of War Henry L. Stimson draws the first name in the selective service lottery.
(Image from the National Archives and Records Administration.)

On August 14, 1941, President Roosevelt eased America away from neutrality by signing the Atlantic Charter with Britain's embattled prime minister, Winston Churchill, aboard the U.S. Navy cruiser *Augusta.*

December 8, 1941: On the day after the Japanese attack against Pearl Harbor, President Roosevelt asked Congress for a declaration of war.
(Image from the National Archives and Records Administration.)

FDR signs the declaration of war voted by Congress. His black armband is a token of mourning for his mother, Sara Delano Roosevelt, who died earlier in the year.
(Image from the National Archives and Records Administration.)

A PERSONAL WORD

"A final personal word. I know that each of you will appreciate that I am speaking no mere politeness when I assure you how much I value the fine relationship that we have shared during these months of hard and incessant work. Out of these friendly contacts we are, fortunately, building a strong and permanent tie between the legislative and executive branches of the government. The letter of the Constitution wisely declared a separation, but the impulse of common purpose declares a union. In this spirit we join once more in serving the American people."

—First annual message to Congress, January 3, 1934

Many business leaders and managers today avoid "getting personal" and insist instead on a sharp division between their business and personal lives. To be sure, the interests of the enterprise do not always coincide with our personal interests; yet it is important always to remember that "business," "the firm," "the department" are fictions constructed around the only reality that finally matters: people—the people who make up the business, the firm, or the department.

A leader leads people, not the "container" in which they happen to find themselves. An effective leader never forgets this and what is more, she never lets the other members of the organization forget that they are being led not by a boss, but by a person. Rather than avoid the personal in business, it is wise, from time to time, to inject a personal note with a "personal word."

In the case of this first annual message to Congress, FDR extended his gratitude to those in the legislature for creating with him a working partnership. Speaking person to person, the president thanked the members of Congress and then reminded them that this person-to-person relationship was in service to their mutual client, "the American people." In this way FDR raised the personal note to a higher level but in so doing, he never let go of the idea that all of this—the leadership, the collaboration, the "fine relationship" between president and Congress—was still a "people" business, a relationship in service to the people of the United States. This realization was the ultimate "personal word."

WHAT I SAW

"I saw drought devastation in nine states."

—Fireside Chat on conservation of natural resources,
September 6, 1936

To his radio audience of September 6, 1936, Roosevelt explained:

> I have been on a journey of husbandry. I went prima-
> rily to see at first hand conditions in the drought states,
> to see how effectively federal and local authorities are
> taking care of pressing problems of relief and also how
> they are to work together to defend the people of this
> country against the effects of future droughts.

Too often executives and managers stay in their offices and behind their desks. They may hear of conditions in the organizations they lead but they do not *see* these conditions for themselves,
at firsthand. Yet there is no substitute for firsthand information
and direct contact. Journeying to gather such information and
make such contact can be time-consuming but it is necessary to
effective leadership.

The simple declarative sentence, "I saw drought devastation in
nine states," speaks volumes. It is very different from saying "Nine

71

states are devastated by drought." This is mere information that can be picked up from a newspaper or the report of some third assistant to an assistant. But to declare that *I saw* the devastation is to convey a world of sympathy and understanding from the very highest level of leadership. FDR bolstered and built on this blockbuster of a sentence by reeling off the particulars:

> I talked with families who had lost their wheat crop, lost their corn crop, lost their livestock, lost the water in their well, lost their garden, and come through to the end of the summer without one dollar of cash resources, facing a winter without feed or food—facing a planting season without seed to put in the ground. . . .
>
> I saw cattlemen who because of lack of grass or lack of winter feed have been compelled to sell all but their breeding stock and will need help to carry even these through the coming winter. I saw livestock kept alive only because water had been brought to them long distances in tank cars. I saw other farm families who have not lost everything but who because they have made only partial crops must have some form of help if they are to continue farming next spring.
>
> I shall never forget the fields of wheat so blasted by heat that they cannot be harvested. I shall never forget field after field of corn stunted, earless and stripped of leaves, for what the sun left the grasshoppers took. I saw brown pastures which would not keep a cow on fifty acres.

Facts vividly rendered but without embellishment are the most effective weapons in a speaker's arsenal. The same is true for a leader. Tell the facts of the matter and you prove, as no other words could prove, that you understand the people you lead. Facts well deployed and clearly expressed are the firmest building blocks of confidence.

Firm and hard as they are, facts may also serve as a springboard for the greatest of leaps of faith. Having rendered a vividly grim picture of Depression-era Dust Bowl America, FDR continued:

> Yet I would not have you think for a single minute that there is permanent disaster in these drought regions, or that the picture I saw meant depopulating these areas. No cracked earth, no blistering sun, no burning wind, no grasshoppers are a permanent match for the indomitable American farmers and stockmen and their wives and children who have carried on through desperate days, and inspire us with their self-reliance, their tenacity, and their courage. It was their fathers' task to make homes; it is their task to keep those homes; it is our task to help them win their fight.

No one would deny that Franklin Roosevelt was an optimist. Yet no one who heard this Fireside Chat, with its detailed picture of drought devastation, could accuse Roosevelt of an optimism founded on ignorance of the facts. Because he rendered so unblinking a picture of the plight of the Dust Bowl farmers, his statement of the "indomitable" spirit of those farmers rings loud and true rather than hollow and false. The leader has seen the terrible facts for himself, he has proven to us that he fully understands them, and he persuades us that they can be overcome. How? Through cooperation between the farmers—whose task it is to keep the homes their fathers built—and the rest of us, whose task it is to help the farmers win their fight.

FDR devoted the rest of this Fireside Chat to outlining the means of furnishing that help through federal programs promoting conservation of natural resources.

STRIKE THE RIGHT TONE

"One up and two to go!"

—Fireside Chat on the Allies' capture of Rome, June 5, 1944

"Yesterday on June 4, 1944, Rome fell to American and Allied troops. The first of the Axis capitals is now in our hands." If the speaker had been a Hitler or even a Stalin, doubtless there would have been much pompous and portentous rhetorical fanfare accompanying this statement. But the speaker was Franklin D. Roosevelt, an American who was keenly in tune with the American attitude toward the task at hand, an attitude of businesslike informality, direct and unencumbered by pomp and circumstance. His next sentence, accordingly, was "One up and two to go!" Rome has been taken; now Berlin must fall and Tokyo, too.

A leader signals in many ways that he is in touch with those he leads: He acknowledges the needs and concerns of the organization. He acknowledges and praises the achievements of the institution. He demonstrates that he shares the values of the organization. And he ensures that he speaks the language of those he leads. This does not mean a foolish display of slang or otherwise talking down to others. Nor does it mean speaking in a way that is foreign to you. To do so comes across as stiff, stilted, and downright phony. But it does mean getting in touch with those elements in your background that you share with others. Fashion your expression from these elements. It will put you in tune with the organization and help to ensure that your message is understood in mind as well as heart.

LAUGHING MATTER

". . . they now include my little dog, Fala."

—Campaign dinner address, September 23, 1944

Late in the summer of 1944 President Roosevelt journeyed to Alaska's Aleutian Islands to visit the army, army air force, and naval personnel stationed in what was perhaps the bleakest outpost of the war. In 1942–43, the Japanese had successfully invaded two of the islands in the Aleutian chain, Kiska and Attu. At the time Alaska, like Hawaii, was a United States territory, not a state, but Kiska and Attu were the only pieces of U.S. territory actually occupied by the Japanese, and driving the invaders out had required a slow and surprisingly bloody campaign. FDR was now eager to pay tribute to the servicemen who had accomplished a vital mission in an obscure corner of the war.

On the return trip from Alaska, a rumor began to circulate that FDR's beloved Scotch terrier, Fala, was accidentally left behind and that Roosevelt had dispatched a U.S. Navy destroyer to retrieve the dog. As rumors inevitably do, this one grew—from a destroyer to a flotilla involving battleships and cruisers. It was bandied about that not only had this sortie cost millions of dollars, but that because vessels were removed from the battle line, a Japanese warship, which might otherwise have been sunk, subsequently attacked and sank an American transport.

Ridiculous though it was, the rumor would not die, and it was even introduced on the floor of the House of Representatives by Congressman Harold Knutson, a Michigan Republican. In response Democratic Majority Leader John McCormack called on northern Pacific commander Admiral William D. Leahy to report the facts. McCormack then read into the *Congressional Record* the admiral's simple declaration: "The dog was never lost."

But then it became FDR's turn to ensure that the rumor was not *quite* laid to rest. In a September 1944 campaign speech to the Teamsters Union in Washington, D.C., Roosevelt addressed what he called "campaign falsifications" issuing from the camp of his opponent, Republican governor of New York Thomas E. Dewey. After listing a number of these "falsifications," FDR reached a climax with "perhaps the most ridiculous . . . one":

> . . . that this Administration failed to prepare for the war that was coming. I doubt whether even [Hitler's propaganda minister Josef] Goebbels would have tried that one. For even he would never have dared hope that the voters of America had already forgotten that many of the Republican leaders in the Congress and outside the Congress tried to thwart and block nearly every attempt that this Administration made to warn our people and to arm our Nation. Some of them called our 50,000 airplane program fantastic. Many of those very same leaders who fought every defense measure that we proposed are still in control of the Republican party—look at their names—were in control of its National Convention in Chicago, and would be in control of the machinery of the Congress and of the

Republican party, in the event of a Republican victory this fall.

FDR could have declared a rhetorical victory right then and marched off the field in triumph and vindication. But the instinct that unerringly drove him to make contact—human, warm, good-humored contact—with his audience would not let him stop quite yet. From the bold calumny that he had failed to prepare for war, FDR turned to a very different accusation:

> These Republican leaders have not been content with attacks on me, or my wife, or on my sons. No, not content with that, they now include my little dog, Fala. Well, of course, I don't resent attacks, and my family doesn't resent attacks, but Fala does resent them. You know, Fala is Scotch, and being a Scottie, as soon as he learned that the Republican fiction writers in Congress and out had concocted a story that I had left him behind on the Aleutian Islands and had sent a destroyer back to find him—at a cost to the taxpayers of two or three, or eight or twenty million dollars—his Scotch soul was furious. He has not been the same dog since. I am accustomed to hearing malicious falsehoods about myself—such as that old, worm-eaten chestnut that I have represented myself as indispensable. But I think I have a right to resent, to object to libelous statements about my dog.

Not only did the teamsters find this brilliant puncturing of campaign rumor and falsehood hilarious, the entire nation did as well, thanks to radio broadcast and newsreel. FDR capped the humor by gently pointing to a serious message behind it: "Well, I think we all recognize the old technique. The people of this country know the past too well to be deceived into forgetting. Too much is at stake to forget. There are tasks ahead of us which we must now complete with the same will and the same skill and intelligence and devotion that have already led us so far along the road to victory."

Franklin Roosevelt defeated Governor Dewey by a margin of 432 electoral votes to 99.

THEME FIVE

ON REFUSING DEFEAT

DEFEAT IS JUST ANOTHER CHOICE

"When you get at the end of your rope, tie a knot and hang on."

—Fireside Chat, April 28, 1935

To the manor born, FDR was nevertheless comfortable with the common man and delighted in speaking his language, but always did so with an eloquence born of gentle directness. He spoke often and much, but he never used ten words when three or four would do. At his best he fashioned incisive phrases that pack the rhetorical punch of a proverb but that are also cloaked in the drama of vivid human dilemma. Here's an example: "When you get at the end of your rope, tie a knot and hang on."

FDR was speaking of his own dilemma as a leader charged with nothing less than the responsibility for reversing the downward spiral of the Great Depression. Yet he used language that alluded not just to his own burden but that also spoke directly to the situation of vast numbers of Americans gathered that evening before their radio sets: By 1935 many of these people had reached the end of their ropes.

A good communicator can talk interestingly about himself. A great communicator can do that *and* make his story the story of his listeners as well.

Leadership is often about finding options when there are none.

To express this, FDR took a well-worn expression of despair—
"I'm at the end of my rope"—and breathed genuine, good-
humored, hopeful life into it. But this act of rhetorical wit also
expressed a simple and profound spiritual truth as well as an immediately practical one. The spiritual message is *never lose hope.*
The practical advice? *Do* something *to survive. Do it precisely when
it seems as if there is nothing you* can *do. And do it with whatever you
happen to have.*

A realistic leader admits when the enterprise has reached the
end of its rope. The choice at that point is whether to let go or
hang on. And that choice is made easier if you can persuade those
you lead that, *Yes, things look bad, but at least we've still got the rope!
The job now is to work with it.*

NO SURRENDER

"We refused to leave the problems of our common welfare to be solved by the winds of chance and the hurricanes of disaster."

—Second inaugural address, January 20, 1937

Success and victory are not always possible, but it does not follow that surrender is the only alternative; at least not the ultimate surrender, which is drift—a surrender to mere chance.

Mistakes are made; things go wrong; disasters happen. No leader can deny this. But a committed leader (and really there can be no other kind) never abandons the enterprise by allowing it to ride with the prevailing current. For each circumstance plans are drawn up, policies determined, and decisions made. Such an approach does not guarantee success but it does reduce the chances for failure and, in the event of failure, tends to reduce its magnitude and impact while increasing the odds of an efficient and timely recovery.

YOU AREN'T DEFEATED
UNTIL YOU GIVE UP

"We have not been stunned. We have not been terrified or confused."

—Ninth annual message to Congress, January 6, 1942

Even in the largest of organizations, the mood of the leader—the CEO, the president, the manager, whoever—percolates through the enterprise. Everyone takes his cue from the feelings communicated by leadership. More often than not, defeatism begins at the top.

An effective leader ensures that the organization knows how he feels and if he wants the organization to prevail, he ensures that the feeling is positive.

This does not require manufacturing a pasteboard smile and a false front. Phony optimism is amazingly transparent. The fact is that communicating a feeling of upbeat confidence calls for squarely facing the very worst that circumstances have to offer and yet demonstrating a refusal to yield to those circumstances.

"The act of Japan at Pearl Harbor," FDR told Congress, "was intended to stun us—to terrify us to such an extent that we would divert our industrial and military strength to the Pacific area, or even to our own continental defense"—and therefore leave Europe to Nazi conquest.

The plan has failed in its purpose. We have not been stunned. We have not been terrified or confused. This very reassembling of the Seventy-seventh Congress today is proof of that; for the mood of quiet, grim resolution which here prevails bodes ill for those who conspired and collaborated to murder world peace.

That mood is stronger than any mere desire for revenge. It expresses the will of the American people to make very certain that the world will never so suffer again.

President Roosevelt did not treat his listeners to the honeyed words of the false optimist but he did project his feelings onto the nation, guiding a response to the disaster that was Pearl Harbor. "We have not been stunned. We have not been terrified or confused," he said. We are not defeated; rather, we are determined to defeat—permanently—Japan and Germany and all they represent.

FDR's leadership message here is a version of what the philosopher Friedrich Nietzsche once said about challenge, injury, and adversity: "What doesn't kill me makes me stronger."

ON PLAIN SPEECH AND GOOD TALK

PAINT A PICTURE

"In a pigeon hole in the desk of the Republican leaders of New York State is a large envelope, soiled, worn and bearing a date that goes back twenty-five years."

—Campaign speech, New York gubernatorial race,
October 20, 1928

So Franklin Roosevelt began his first gubernatorial campaign speech: not by introducing himself, not by greeting his audience, not by saying "We have a problem," but by painting a picture with the brushwork of an elaborate figure of speech:

> In a pigeon hole in the desk of the Republican leaders of New York State is a large envelope, soiled, worn and bearing a date that goes back twenty-five years. Printed in large letters on this envelope are the words "Promises to Labor." Inside the envelope are a series of sheets dated two years apart and representing the best thought of the best minds of the Republican leaders over the succession of years. Each sheet of promises is practically a duplicate of every other sheet. Nowhere in that envelope is there a single page bearing the title "Promises Kept."

91

If candidate Roosevelt had simply claimed that New York's Republican leaders don't keep their promises to labor, he would have been just one more candidate making one more claim. Instead he created a memorable word portrait of twenty-five years of broken promises. Leadership is not about commanding obedience. It is about persuasion, the winning of hearts and minds. Often the most effective way to appeal to those hearts and minds is to create a vivid picture of reality—even if that picture exists wholly in the imagination.

EXPLAIN IT

"I want to talk for a few minutes with the people of the United States about banking . . ."

—Fireside Chat on the banking crisis, March 12, 1933

Franklin Roosevelt brought to the American presidency a new, intensely personal dimension. Those who lived during the Roosevelt years always speak of the feeling they had that FDR was *their* president. This was no accident but was in large part the result of the president's unique—and unprecedented—communication style. As governor of New York, FDR realized the tremendous power and reach of the new mass-communication medium of broadcast radio. The very first commercial radio broadcast had been made in 1920 from station KDKA in Pittsburgh. By the beginning of the 1930s it was the rare American family that didn't own or otherwise have access to a radio. Roosevelt addressed the people of New York State over the radio, and at the end of his first week as president of the United States, on Sunday, March 12, 1933, he delivered on radio a talk from the Diplomatic Reception Room of the White House. It was the first of twenty-seven broadcasts FDR would make during his presidency.

For the March broadcast and for those that followed, "talk" is a more appropriate term than the formal-sounding "address," but the phrase that was ultimately applied to the radio speeches (first used by CBS executive Harry C. Butcher at the time of the second broadcast, May 7, 1933) is far more expressive than either term: Fireside Chat.

Radio, FDR realized, was an intimate medium that literally brought speakers—entertainers, world leaders, it didn't matter who—into the same parlors in which families across America visited with their friends and neighbors. Roosevelt saw the vehicle of the Fireside Chat as a powerful way to explain his economic policies and political programs directly to the people, one on one. There was no reporter's filtering sensibility intervening, and there was no need for the sometimes intimidating formality of a political speech.

Roosevelt's usual tactic was to speak on a single issue of pressing importance for fifteen but no more than thirty minutes. He tried to schedule each Fireside Chat on a Sunday evening, when most people were at home, together as a family, and when audiences were at their biggest—30 to 40 million at a time when the United States population numbered about 130 million. The spontaneous, conversational tone of the Fireside Chats was actually a carefully crafted effect, as FDR and his staff meticulously prepared each chat through draft after draft. What was never contrived, however, was the buoyant optimism that drove most of the chats.

The first Fireside Chat, on March 12, 1933, focused on an issue of intense and immediate concern to Americans, the banking crisis. Financial panic had caused a nationwide epidemic of runs on banks as worried depositors rushed to get at their savings before their bank followed others in failure. For most working men and women the local bank was nothing more or less than a safe place to keep money. The impression was that one's money was safely tucked away in a vault and could be had on demand. In fact, as FDR explained in this Fireside Chat, "the bank does not put the money into a safe deposit vault. It invests your money in many different forms of credit. . . . A comparatively small part of the money you put into the bank is kept in currency—an amount which in normal times is wholly sufficient to cover the cash needs of the average citizen." February and early March 1933, however, were not "normal times," and, as FDR continued, "there was a general rush by a large portion of our population to turn bank deposits into currency or gold—a rush so great that the soundest banks could not get enough currency to meet the demand." Why not? "The reason for this was that on the spur of the moment it was, of course, impossible to sell perfectly sound assets of a bank and convert them into cash except at panic prices far below their real value. By the afternoon of March third scarcely a bank in the country was open to do business."

FDR had coped with the banking crisis by calling a special session of Congress, through which the president ushered the Emergency Banking Act, the most important feature of which was a bank holiday, instituted on March 6. The temporary closure of the nation's banks gave them some breathing space and enabled examiners to separate solvent banks from insolvent ones. FDR used this Fireside Chat to explain the purpose of the bank holiday and to detail the schedule under which sound banks would reopen the following week. His explanation was straightforward and thoroughly honest. His belief was that if the people understood the banking crisis and what was being done about it, they would heed his plea to remain calm. FDR was right. Not only did the nation's solvent banks reopen according to the schedule he outlined, but within a few days deposits were outstripping withdrawals. The banking crisis had been successfully managed.

This first Fireside Chat contained no lofty rhetoric, no lecturing, just the honesty and clarity of a leader speaking to the people as one citizen to another:

> I want to talk for a few minutes with the people of the
> United States about banking—with the comparatively

few who understand the mechanics of banking but more particularly with the overwhelming majority who use banks for the making of deposits and the drawing of checks. I want to tell you what has been done in the last few days, why it was done, and what the next steps are going to be.

The subject and intention of the talk could not have been expressed more clearly. Now FDR struck his typical note of inclusiveness:

I recognize that the many proclamations from State Capitols and from Washington, the legislation, the Treasury regulations, etc., couched for the most part in banking and legal terms should be explained for the benefit of the average citizen. I owe this in particular because of the fortitude and good temper with which everybody has accepted the inconvenience and hardships of the banking holiday. I know that when you understand what we in Washington have been about I shall continue to have your cooperation as fully as I have had your sympathy and help during the past week.

Nowhere does the president say "you must"; nowhere did he take the compliance of the American people for granted. Instead he declared, "I owe" an explanation "because of the fortitude and good temper with which everybody has accepted the inconvenience and hardships of the banking holiday." He acknowledged the sacrifices that have been made and he expressed his belief that when people fully understand the reason for those sacrifices—and the value they have bought—"I shall continue to have your cooperation as fully as I have had your sympathy and help during the past week." Good leadership is always a sound contract with those you lead.

LEADERSHIP BY SIMILE

"The job of creating a program for the nation's welfare is, in some respects, like the building of a ship."

—Fireside Chat on the Works Relief Program,
April 28, 1935

Who is not familiar with the threadbare cliché that tells us "one picture is worth a thousand words"? And who can disagree?

Yet real visual aids are not always necessary to effective leadership communication. The most compelling messages are delivered neither in actual pictures nor in abstract words but in language that evokes concrete, familiar reality. This is the language of simile and metaphor, words that create images to appeal directly to the imagination. For communicating ideas with precision and emotional impact, such language is even more effective than a literal picture and certainly more powerful than some dry-as-dust academic and theoretical discussion.

All too often, however, similes and metaphors are carelessly tossed into a speech as mere window dressing. FDR never wasted valuable words and valuable time in such foolishness. Instead his proposition—"The job of creating a program for the nation's welfare is, in some respects, like the building of a ship"—is intensely

97

provocative. It is a classic hook by which the speaker grabs us. We naturally want to know: Just *how* is this one thing like the other? And so we listen more intently:

> At different points on the coast where I often visit they build great seagoing ships. When one of these ships is under construction and the steel frames have been set in the keel it is difficult for a person who does not know ships to tell how it will finally look when it is sailing the high seas.
>
> It may seem confused to some, but out of the multitude of detailed parts that go into the making of the structure, the creation of a useful instrument for man ultimately comes.

So now we have a picture. FDR takes us by the hand, as it were, to a shipyard and, with a few deft words, conjures up the image of a ship just beginning construction. To the uninitiated—most of us—the object on the ways hardly resembles a ship. How, we may wonder, can anyone expect this ever to sail? And yet sail it will: "out of the multitude of detailed parts . . . a useful instrument for man ultimately comes." Strange and confusing as the first framework may look, there is not the slightest doubt that it will, when complete, be a ship "sailing the high seas."

Having created this image, Roosevelt shifts to the point of it all:

> It is that way with the making of a national policy. The objective of the nation has greatly changed in three years [since FDR took office]. Before that time individual self-interest and group selfishness were paramount in public thinking. The general good was at a discount.
>
> Three years of hard thinking have changed the picture. More and more people, because of clearer think-

ing and a better understanding, are considering the
whole rather than a mere part relating to one [geo-
graphical] section, or to one crop, or to one industry,
or to an individual private occupation.

Through looking at the framework of a program for national welfare under construction, FDR explains, more and more people are
capable of seeing beyond the disparate nuts and bolts of legislation and regulation to glimpse the structure that is taking shape
and which, like a great ship, will sail the nation out of the drydock
of Depression. To be sure, if you focus on this or that part, the final form is not apparent. But if you imagine how each part contributes to the whole, you cannot but have faith that this structure
will indeed sail: our new ship of state.

DEFINE YOUR TERMS

"Democracy, the practice of self-government, is a covenant among free men to respect the rights and liberties of their fellows."

—Sixth annual message to Congress, January 4, 1939

Effective communication, which is essential to effective leadership, depends on clarity; command of the facts of the situation; eloquence; sincerity; and passion. But none of these qualities means much if the speaker uses a language the audience does not understand.

Any project, undertaking, or enterprise is centered on certain key concepts and terms. Usually such concepts and terms relate to goals or guiding principles. It is a common leadership mistake to assume that all members of the enterprise are familiar with the key terms and concepts and fully understand them as the leader intends them to be understood. Avoid this mistake by defining the key concepts of your message.

Here, in addressing Congress at a time of grave international peril, when Nazi Germany, fascist Italy, and militarist Japan menaced the world, FDR eloquently defined *democracy,* along with *religion* and *international good faith* as the three cornerstones of "modern civilization" and the three values on which America and

American international policy are built. The definitions were *not* drawn from any dictionary. They were personal rather than lexicographical, relating most directly to values: "Democracy, the practice of self-government, is a covenant among free men to respect the rights and liberties of their fellows." Always emphasizing cooperation and respect, FDR defined *democracy* not in terms of one's personal liberty, but as respect for the rights and liberties of others. It was a distinctly unselfish definition, which, if universally observed, would ensure personal liberty for every individual.

Likewise FDR's definition of religion was functional rather than static. Roosevelt was not interested in what religion *is,* but in what it *does:* "Religion, by teaching man his relationship to God, gives the individual a sense of his own dignity and teaches him to respect himself by respecting his neighbors."

The president added to this *international good faith,* "a sister of democracy," which "springs from the will of civilized nations of men to respect the rights and liberties of other nations of men."

What ties all three concepts and definitions together is the common thread of respect for the rights and liberties of others. Superficially, the message here is typical of FDR: a call for self-sacrifice. But dig a little deeper, and it becomes clear that only through such apparent *self-sacrifice* can we hope to obtain *self-fulfillment.* Rights and liberties are not taken, but given. We give them to one another. Only if everyone in the enterprise gives this gift does anyone in the enterprise truly enjoy it. That is the nature of a democratic society and of any organization built along democratic lines.

It is the leader's job to make this truth real for those she leads: that respect enables respect; that honoring the liberty of another creates a free society for you, for everyone; and that rights are always given—never taken.

"Above all," Roosevelt continued farther on in the speech, "we have made the American people conscious of their interrelationship and their interdependence. They sense a common destiny and a common need of each other. Differences of occupation, geography, race, and religion no longer obscure the nation's fundamental unity in thought and in action."

A consciousness of interrelationship and interdependence, of a common destiny, a common need of each other, a fundamental unity: What CEO, manager, or supervisor would wish for anything less than this?

DEFINE THE CHALLENGE

"We face one of the great choices in history."

—Radio address to the 1940 Democratic National
Convention, July 19, 1940

Think of the leader as a definer.

The world of 1940 was a world at war. The only major power not yet engaged in actual combat was the United States. Viewing the situation of 1940 through the hindsight of history, it is difficult to imagine that any American could have hoped to stay out of the war. Yet until the attack on Pearl Harbor on December 7, 1941, many, perhaps most, Americans sincerely believed that was possible.

Although he was an optimist, FDR was first and foremost a realist. "I do not regret my consistent endeavor to awaken this country to the menace for us and for all we hold dear," he said in his radio address. "I have pursued these efforts in the face of appeaser fifth columnists who charged me with hysteria and warmongering. But I felt it my duty—my simple, plain, inescapable duty—to arouse my countrymen to the danger of the new forces let loose in the world."

What FDR articulated were the duties of every leader: to recognize the nature of the current situation and to define, for the entire enterprise, the challenges posed by that situation. In his radio address, Roosevelt listed them:

> We face one of the great choices of history.
>   It is not alone a choice of government by the people versus dictatorship.
>   It is not alone a choice of freedom versus slavery.
>   It is not alone a choice between moving forward or falling back.
>   It is all of these rolled into one.
>   It is the continuance of civilization as we know it versus the ultimate destruction of all that we have held dear—religion against godlessness; the ideal of justice against the practice of force; moral decency versus the firing squad; courage to speak out, and to act, versus the false lullaby of appeasement.

A nameless menace brings sheer terror. Define that menace and, no matter how terrible, it may now be confronted in a spirit of hope, of the possibility of solution. Looking upon the terrifying world of 1940, FDR reduced its terrors to a set of simply stated, but very powerful, choices, which offered no middle ground. While the consequences of the choices, FDR knew, would be arduous, making the choices, once they were stated clearly, would be straightforward for most Americans. For he defined the present challenge as a choice between losing all that means anything to us or taking the actions necessary to preserve all that means everything to us.

SHINE A NEW LIGHT

"America has adopted Selective Service in time of peace, and, in doing so, has broadened and enriched our basic concept of citizenship."

—Statement on the adoption of peacetime selective service, September 16, 1940

Menaced by a world at war, the United States Congress, at President Roosevelt's urging, enacted the first peacetime military draft (selective service) in national history. This momentous step prompted FDR to present himself fully as what today's political pundits would call a "spin doctor."

A spin doctor's practice consists of putting a positive "spin" on actions bound to stir negative feelings. As most of us interpret it, the term is pejorative, implying distortion of the truth. Yet it is often the leader's task, for the benefit of the organization he leads, to shine a new light on necessary evils and reveal them as necessary goods or, at the very least, as necessary, period. Thus it was with the peacetime draft. On the face of it, what young man wanted to be *compelled* to leave hearth, home, family, and job for a stint in the army? Yet the survival of the nation depended on rapidly building up an army, and this had to be accomplished faster and to a greater extent than ordinary recruitment and voluntary enlistment could accomplish.

So FDR jumped in without apology, without allusion to grim necessity, but with words like *broadened* and *enriched*—positive language that any master salesman would be comfortable with:

> America has adopted Selective Service in time of peace, and, in doing so, has broadened and enriched our basic concept of citizenship. Beside the clear democratic ideals of equal rights, equal privileges, and equal opportunities, we have set forth the underlying other duties, obligations, and responsibilities of equal service.

The spin is ultra positive: the draft is an opportunity to realize the full spectrum of U.S. citizenship.

Having cast the legislation in a new light, FDR progressed to the next rhetorical leadership step, persuading his audience that this bold innovation is not really new at all. This was a familiar leadership exercise for FDR, who, since 1933, had been easing Americans into acceptance of the new, the unfamiliar, even the radical by persuasively demonstrating the links between each innovation and American tradition and precedent:

> In thus providing for national defense, we have not carved a new and uncharted trail in the history of our democratic institutions. On the contrary, we have merely reasserted an old and accepted principle of democratic government. The militia system, the self-armed citizenry with the obligation of military service incumbent upon every free man, has its roots in the old common law. . . . At the time of the adoption of the federal Constitution, nine of the thirteen states explicitly provided for universal service in their basic laws.

Of course, Roosevelt went on to explain, technological circumstances have changed since the eighteenth century. "In those days, little was required in the way of equipment and training for the man in arms. The average American had his flintlock and knew how to use it. . . . Today, the art of war calls for a wide variety of technical weapons. Modern life does not emphasize the qualities demanded of soldiers." Thus, the aim of selective service was to create an army fit to fight a modern war, providing equipment, training, and physical conditioning. "Moreover, behind the armed forces, we must have a munitions industry as a part of an economic system capable of providing the fighting man with his full requirements of arms and equipment. Many individuals, therefore, may serve their country best by holding their posts on the production line." Another function of selective service was to make this determination equitably and efficiently.

After shining a new light on the peacetime draft, then setting it into historical context, comparing and contrasting the traditions of yesterday with the needs of today, FDR went on to explain, clearly and concisely, just how the selective service system would operate. This done, he once again shone that new light with a concluding sentence: "Universal service will bring not only greater preparedness to meet the threat of war, but a wider distribution of tolerance and understanding to enjoy the blessings of peace."

GET DOWN TO BUSINESS

"I want to talk to you about rubber—about rubber and the war—about rubber and the American people."

—Radio address on the scrap rubber campaign,
June 12, 1942

Sometimes leaders talk about ideas, about goals, about inspiration, about commitment. Sometimes they talk about rubber.

Too many leaders are afraid to roll up their sleeves and dig into the nitty-gritty of their enterprise. They fear being accused of micromanaging, of getting bogged down in the details. And that *can* happen. But there are details and then there are the *key* details on which enterprises rise or fall. Effective leadership calls for a practiced ability to distinguish between the myriad details that can and should be entrusted to subordinates and those few key details that require hands-on attention.

FDR recognized rubber as one of these key details. He was not afraid to turn from lofty speeches concerning democracy and sacrifice to talk about rubber—"about rubber and the war—about rubber and the American people."

> When I say rubber I mean rubber. I don't mean gasoline. Gasoline is a serious problem only in certain sections of the country.

But rubber is a problem everywhere—from one end of the country to the other—in the Mississippi Valley as well as in the East, in the oil country as well as in the corn country or the iron country or the great industrial centers.

Rubber is a problem for this reason: because modern wars cannot be won without rubber and because 92 percent of our normal supply of rubber has been cut off by the Japanese.

That is serious. It would be more serious if we had not built up a stockpile of rubber before the war started, if we were not now building up a great new synthetic rubber industry. That takes time, so we have an immediate need.

Examine this passage carefully. It states its subject in no uncertain terms: rubber—not gasoline. It goes on to explain, very specifically, why rubber is a problem: modern wars cannot be won without rubber, and the Japanese have cut off 92 percent of our normal supply. This sounds quite dire: to be deprived of 92 percent of something needed to win the war! But having gotten his listeners' attention, FDR presented some of the ameliorating circumstances that made the situation a bit less alarming: We have a stockpile, and we are developing a "great new" synthetic rubber industry. This said, he went on to explain that creating a new industry takes time, so "we have an immediate need." He continued:

Neither the stockpile, nor the synthetic plants which are now being built, nor both together will be enough to provide for the needs of our great new army and navy plus our civilian requirements as they now exist.

The armed services have done what they can. They have eliminated rubber wherever possible. The army, for example, has had to replace rubber treads with less efficient steel treads on many of its tanks. Army and navy estimates of use of rubber have had to be curtailed all along the line.

The president presented relevant details on military conservation of rubber—conservation measures, he deftly pointed out, that involved some sacrifice of optimum efficiency. So, as he further observed: "there is a limit" to what the military can sacrifice. After all, "You and I want the finest and most efficient army and navy the world has ever seen—an army and navy with the greatest and swiftest striking power. That means rubber—huge quantities of rubber—rubber for trucks and tanks and planes and gun mounts, rubber for gas masks and rubber for landing boats." FDR added that rubber was essential not just to the instruments of war, but to the *production* of those instruments. "All this adds up to a very serious problem," he declares, "a problem we will solve."

> But there is one unknown factor in this problem. We know what our stockpile is. We know what our synthetic capacity will be. But we do not know how much used rubber there is in the country—used rubber which, reclaimed and reprocessed, can be combined with our supplies of new rubber to make those supplies go farther in meeting military and civilian needs.
>
> Specifically, we don't know how much used rubber there is in your cellar—your barn—your stockroom—your garage—your attic.
>
> There are as many opinions as there are experts, and until we know we can't make our plans for the best use of the rubber we have. The only way to find out is to get the used rubber in where it can stand up and be counted.
>
> And that precisely is what we propose to do.

The president of the United States, one of the two leaders of the free world, went on to detail the mechanics of the scrap rubber drive—what was needed and where to bring it. Neighborhood filling stations agreed to serve as collection points for the scrap rubber during a specified collection period. "If you think it is rubber," FDR requested, "take it to your nearest filling station. Once the rubber is in, we will know what our supplies of used rubber are and we will make our plans accordingly."

Having narrowed his focus and that of his listeners to the subject of rubber and to what each individual listening to his voice could do to increase America's store of rubber, Roosevelt suddenly connected this detail to the big picture:

> One thing you can be sure of: we are going to see to it that there is enough rubber to build the planes to bomb Tokyo and Berlin—enough rubber to build the tanks to crush the enemy wherever we may find him— enough rubber to win the war.

No danger of micromanagement here. Instead the president made a sweeping, seamless connection between a scrap of rubber and total victory.

MAKE SENSE

"I want to make a personal report to you . . ."

—Address before Congress on the Yalta Conference,
March 1, 1945

The Yalta Conference was the last meeting with the Allied leaders, Winston Churchill and Josef Stalin, that Franklin Roosevelt attended before his death of a cerebral hemorrhage on April 12, 1945. This report to Congress on the conference was his final speech. Those who saw the president deliver it were shocked by his gaunt appearance and doubtless they were dismayed that, for the first time, the polio-stricken chief executive did not stand to deliver the address. ("I hope," he began, "you will pardon me for this unusual posture of sitting down during the presentation of what I want to say, but I know that you will realize it makes it a lot easier for me not to have to carry about ten pounds of steel around on the bottom of my legs; and also because of the fact that I have just completed a fourteen-thousand-mile trip.") They missed, too, the customary jaunty vigor of voice. And yet the content was as strong, compelling, and well-reasoned as ever. Consider the following paragraphs. A few words and phrases have been italicized to draw your attention to them:

It has been a long journey. I hope you will also agree that it has been, so far, a fruitful one.

Speaking in all frankness, the question of whether it is entirely fruitful or not lies to a great extent *in your hands*. For unless you here in the halls of the American Congress—with the support of the American people—concur in the general conclusions reached at Yalta, and give them your active support, the meeting will not have produced lasting results.

That is why I have come before you at the earliest hour I could after my return. I want to make *a personal report to you*—and, at the same time, to the people of the country. Many months of earnest work are ahead of us all, and I should like to feel that when the last stone is laid on the structure of international peace, it will be an achievement for which *all of us* in America have worked steadfastly and unselfishly—*together.*

I am returning from this trip—that took me so far—refreshed and inspired. I was well the entire time. I was not ill for a second, until I arrived back in Washington, and there I heard all of the rumors which had occurred in my absence. I returned from the trip refreshed and inspired. The Roosevelts are not, as you may suspect, averse to travel. We seem to thrive on it!

Far away as I was, I was kept constantly informed of affairs in the United States. The modern miracles of rapid communication have made this world very small. We must always bear in mind that fact, when we speak or think of international relations. I received a steady stream of messages from Washington—I might say from not only the executive branch with all its departments, but also from the legislative branch—and except where radio silence was necessary for security purposes, I could continuously send messages any place in the world. And of course, in a grave emergency, we could have even risked the breaking of the security rule.

I come from the Crimea Conference with a firm belief that we have made a good start on the road to a world of peace. *There were two main purposes in* this Crimea Conference. *The first was* to bring defeat to Germany with the greatest possible speed, and the smallest possible loss of Allied men. *That purpose is now being carried out* in great force. The German army and the German people, are feeling the ever increasing might of our fighting men and of the Allied armies. Every hour gives us added pride in the heroic advance of our troops in Germany—on German soil—toward a meeting with the gallant Red Army.

The second purpose was to continue to build the foundation for an international accord that would bring order and security after the chaos of the war, that would give some assurance of lasting peace among the nations of the world.

Toward that goal also, a tremendous stride was made.

The words emphasized with italics are not beautiful nouns or flowery adjectives. They are not great passages of descriptive prose. They are the simple, straightforward signposts of effective, muscular English.

FDR made clear that he had done his exhausting utmost in traveling to Yalta in the far-off Crimea to discuss with the Allied leaders the end of the war and the beginning of the postwar world. Now the results are *"in your hands,"* he told Congress. To ensure that the United States would act on the substance of the Yalta Conference, he said, *"that is why* I have come before you." How important is all this? Important enough that "I want to make *a personal report to you*—and, at the same time, to the people of the country." Whose achievement is the "structure of international peace" begun at the Yalta Conference? "It will be an achievement for which *all of us* in America have worked steadfastly and unselfishly—*together.*"

The use of simple, forceful, direction-pointing words and phrases delivers the message with unmistakable energy. He continued:

> *There were two main purposes* in this Crimea Conference. *The first was* to bring defeat to Germany with the greatest possible speed, and the smallest possible loss of Allied men. *That purpose is now being carried out* in great force.

Effective leadership communication is all about making promises and delivering on them. The phrase *"there were two main purposes"* promised to tell the audience about two main purposes. FDR immediately made good on the promise: *"The first was . . ."* And he went on to give a capsule report on the status of this first purpose: *"That purpose is now being carried out* in great force." From here, he continued:

> *The second purpose was* to continue to build the foundation for an international accord that would bring order and security after the chaos of the war, that would give some assurance of lasting peace among the nations of the world.
>
> *Toward that goal also,* a tremendous stride was made.

The second pledge was thus redeemed, and, as with the first, FDR added a status report: *"Toward that goal also, a tremendous stride was made."*

Persuasive leadership communication does not require elo-

quence borrowed from a thesaurus. It does call for a clear understanding of what you are about, of purpose, of objectives, of goals,
and of means, methods, and resources. Then it further calls for a
forceful and unambiguous presentation of each of these elements.
Fancy words and linguistic sleight of hand are neither necessary
nor, for that matter, helpful. Instead use the simplest language
compatible with the complexity of your message. Identify purpose, objectives, goals, means, methods, and resources, then point
your listeners' or readers' way to each of these and from one to the
next. Whatever else a leader does, a leader must make sense.

ON PREPARATION
AND RISK

HEART

"Governments can err, presidents do make mistakes, but the immortal Dante tells us that Divine justice weighs the sins of the cold-blooded and the sins of the warm-hearted in different scales."

—Speech before the 1936 Democratic National Convention, June 27, 1936

To lead—indeed, to take action—is to risk failure and error. Not that inaction or the absence of leadership brings safety, but leaders are necessarily risk takers. No one was more aware than Franklin Roosevelt, running for a second term, that his first term as president had been packed with action. The celebrated first hundred days saw the introduction of a dazzling array of executive orders, programs, and legislative initiatives aimed at alleviating the economic disasters of the Great Depression.

Not all of them succeeded. Not everyone was happy with the results of each and every thing the president did or sponsored. But FDR never sought to backpedal or disavow his failures and disappointments. Instead he explained them as products of a necessary impulse: heart or "Charity—in the true spirit of that grand old word. For charity literally translated from the original means love, the love that understands, that does not merely share the wealth of the giver, but in true sympathy and wisdom helps men to help themselves."

> We seek not merely to make government a mechanical implement, but to give it the vibrant personal character that is the very embodiment of human charity. . . . Better the occasional faults of a government that lives in a spirit of charity than the consistent omissions of a government frozen in the ice of its own indifference.

Good government—or effective leadership—is not about avoiding errors but about engaging the needs of the people who make up the organization and enterprise. The most fulfilling way in which to engage these needs is on a personal, feeling, responsive level, a level of sympathy, of true understanding: the level of the heart. To adopt any other approach, an approach less human and more businesslike, misses the deepest purpose of leadership, which is always, somehow, to improve life and lives. Failing to keep this ultimate purpose uppermost in mind results in a government, organization, or leadership "frozen in the ice of its own indifference."

BETWEEN PANIC AND ACTION

"I have recently pointed out how quickly the tempo of modern warfare could bring into our very midst the physical attack which we must eventually expect if the dictator nations win this war."

—Eighth annual message to Congress, January 6, 1941

The situation of Europe and the world was desperate indeed at the start of January 1941. America was not yet in the war, but FDR knew that it could not stay out much longer. A vital function of good leadership is the ability to recognize oncoming danger. But even more important is what the leader does when she sees something threatening on the horizon. Does she create panic within the organization? Or does she direct effective action? On the cusp of danger, good leadership consists in navigating a rapid course between panic and action.

In this speech to Congress, FDR urged readiness for war, beginning with the enactment of what would come to be called a lend-lease program: "I recommend that we make it possible for those nations [vital to our defense] to obtain war materials in the United States, fitting their orders into our own program." He then went on to present a complete program for increased war production and for the rapid expansion of the army and navy.

In all this, Roosevelt knew he would meet resistance from those who feared that preparing for war would propel us into war. To overcome the resistance, the president sold his program of action by painting a vivid picture of the clear and present dangers facing the nation:

> Armed defense of democratic existence is now being gallantly waged in four continents. If that defense fails, all the population and all the resources of Europe, Asia, Africa, and Australasia will be dominated by the conquerors. Let us remember that the total of those populations and their resources in those four continents greatly exceeds the sum total of the population and the resources of the whole of the Western Hemisphere—many times over.
>
> In times like these it is immature—and incidentally, untrue—for anybody to brag that an unprepared America, singlehanded, and with one hand tied behind its back, can hold off the whole world.
>
> No realistic American can expect from a dictator's peace international generosity, or return of true independence, or world disarmament, or freedom of expression, or freedom of religion—or even good business. . . .
>
> I have recently pointed out how quickly the tempo of modern warfare could bring into our very midst the physical attack which we must eventually expect if the dictator nations win this war.
>
> There is much loose talk of our immunity from immediate and direct invasion from across the seas. Obviously, as long as the British navy retains its power, no such danger exists. Even if there were no British navy, it is not probable that any enemy would be stupid enough to attack us by landing troops in the United

States from across thousands of miles of ocean, until it
had acquired strategic bases from which to operate.

In this account of a world in turmoil and a nation in imminent
peril there is no hyperbolic language and no words calculated
merely to instill fear. But FDR did let the facts speak for themselves.

First, defenders of democracy are fighting tyrannical aggression in four continents. If they fail in this defense, the United
States will be at the mercy of the "populations and . . . resources
of four continents," which "greatly exceed[ ] the sum total of the
population and resources of the whole of the Western Hemisphere—many times over."

Second, we cannot expect an unprepared America to hold off
the onslaught of the world.

Third, it is folly to put confidence in the generosity of a "dictator's peace."

Fourth, if the "dictator nations" prevail against those nations
that currently oppose them, "we must . . . expect" a "physical attack."

Fifth, despite "loose talk" of "immunity from . . . invasion
from across the seas," such an invasion is quite possible, if the aggression of the "dictator nations" is allowed to prevail.

The surest course between panic and action is defined by facts,
and that is what FDR methodically presented here. He did not
embellish those facts, but neither did he muffle or disguise them.
These facts were the foundation from which he asked Congress to
give him the legislative tools and the money needed to prepare for
dangers that, while all too real, were not insurmountable, provided that timely preparations were made.

MAKE THE PRESENT DANGER CLEAR

"The war is approaching the brink of the Western Hemisphere itself. It is coming very close to home."

—Radio address announcing an unlimited national emergency, May 27, 1941

To motivate his countrymen to accept and endorse preparations for war, including his declaration of an unlimited national emergency, Franklin Roosevelt not only outlined in clear, vivid terms the recent course of Nazi aggression but demonstrated how readily Nazi aggression, if unchecked, could close in on the Americas:

> [The Nazis] . . . have the armed power at any moment to occupy Spain and Portugal; and that threat extends not only to French North Africa and the western end of the Mediterranean but it extends also to the Atlantic fortress of Dakar, and to the island outposts of the New World—the Azores and Cape Verde Islands.
>
> The Cape Verde Islands are only seven hours' distance from Brazil by bomber or troop-carrying planes. They dominate shipping routes to and from the South Atlantic.

The war is approaching the brink of the Western Hemisphere itself. It is coming very close to home.

This is a picture—a motion picture, really, an action movie—of approaching danger. It is rendered not in abstract speculation, but in terms of real places in the real world. A leader needs to keep the focus of everyone on reality, reality founded on what *is* happening and what present events imply about the future. For those who still might close their eyes to the movie FDR reels out, he offers a see-for-yourself approach:

> Anyone with an atlas, anyone with a reasonable knowledge of the sudden striking force of modern war, knows that it is stupid to wait until a probable enemy has gained a foothold from which to attack. Old-fashioned common sense calls for the use of a strategy that will prevent such an enemy from gaining a foothold in the first place.

Roosevelt invited action (look at an atlas) and thought (ponder the "sudden striking force of modern war"). Do this, ponder that, and the conclusion, he implied, is inescapable: The United States is not isolated and insulated from the war that is now taking place. The movie has begun. The film is running.

Having made the present danger clear to his audience, the American people and the Pan-American Union, FDR went on to outline the steps that are being taken to meet this danger. The two paragraphs that follow turn on the word "accordingly":

> We have, accordingly, extended our patrol in North and South Atlantic waters. We are steadily adding more and more ships and planes to that patrol. It is well known that the strength of the Atlantic Fleet has

been greatly increased during the past year, and that it is constantly being built up.

These ships and planes warn of the presence of attacking raiders, on the sea, under the sea, and above the sea. The danger from these raiders is, of course, greatly lessened if their location is definitely known. We are thus being forewarned. We shall be on our guard against efforts to establish Nazi bases closer to our hemisphere.

Sometimes a leader must make clear a present danger, but it is destructive folly to do so without also providing, at the very least, a direction for defense.

THEME EIGHT

ON CHANGE

PAY YOUR DEBTS

"This day is notable not so much for the inauguration of a new governor as that it marks the close of the term of a governor who has been our chief executive for eight years."

—First gubernatorial inaugural address,
Albany, January 1, 1929

The hallmark of an FDR speech is a provocative opening. Whether provocative of thought, enthusiasm, agreement, or dispute, the first words out of FDR's mouth typically provoke the engagement of the audience. We're hooked, one way or another.

Of the many themes that enter and reenter the leadership career of Franklin Roosevelt, none is clearer or more insistent than the theme of engagement—this leader's refusal to permit those he leads to remain passive or detached. And so it is with the opening sentence of FDR's first gubernatorial inaugural address, given at Albany on January 1, 1929. Roosevelt, the incoming governor, did not merely acknowledge or even give credit to outgoing governor Al Smith, but invited his audience to dedicate *this* day, inauguration day, to Smith.

Spoken by a less skillful communicator or a less effective leader, such an opening would have been an unbecoming display of excessive humility—hardly a promising beginning for a new chief executive. But FDR used the sentence as a springboard to a speech about taking New York State to ever loftier heights through a combination of willing self-sacrifice and innovative thinking. He began, however, by paying a debt to Governor Smith, a "public servant of true greatness." By giving Smith his due and more, FDR conveyed to those he was about to lead, the people of New York, that they have made an eight-year investment in the programs of Al Smith and that he, Franklin D. Roosevelt, as the new governor, intended to capitalize on that investment, to build on it, to grow it in new directions, yes, but in directions based on the original down payment.

As a leader FDR was a great innovator. Some thought him a radical. Yet he was always careful to separate innovation from radicalism. Radicalism departs sharply from what has come before, whereas innovation builds on it. Even if the innovator travels very far from the starting point, there is always a clearly discernible route back to that starting point, a thread of tradition. It is this connection, FDR recognized, that allows most people to accept new ideas. This speech is vintage Roosevelt, Roosevelt as the pioneer, the leader into uncharted territory. *I will take you to new places,* Roosevelt promised, but he always added to the promise: *I will take you to new places, just as other successful American leaders have done before.* Governor Al Smith, the argument of this speech goes, innovated your government, and you have invested in those innovations. Join me in building on that investment and continuing the innovation.

So FDR began this inaugural speech, a speech about a beginning, by paying a debt, something owed for something already done, and he did so in the knowledge that a debt paid is really an investment in the future.

INNOVATE FROM THE ROOTS UP

"What is the State?"

> —Message to the New York State legislature,
> August 28, 1931

The expression "think outside the box" has become a well-worn cliché. Yet it is still a provocative saying. That is, if someone says "think outside of the box," it is difficult to resist a kind of natural urge to crane the neck and squint the eyes in order to catch a peek outside or around the box—whatever "the box" is.

Think outside of the box. Fine. But how?

There is a sure way to begin, and that is not to *think* at all but to *rethink*. Take a fresh look at the elements of an issue or problem, the very components you take for granted, to which, ordinarily, you wouldn't give thought at all. Now reexamine those elements. Rethink them. Rethink their nature, their strengths, their weaknesses, their purpose. Having rethought the elements, use them to approach the problem or issue at hand.

This is thinking outside of the box.

In introducing a radical and unprecedented program of state-funded measures to address the Great Depression, Governor Franklin Roosevelt sought to overcome the resistance of the legislature by inviting the members to rethink the most basic element with which, for which, and in which they worked: "What is the State?" his speech began:

> It is the duly constituted representative of an organized society of human beings, created by them for their mutual protection and well-being. "The State" or "The Government" is but the machinery through which such mutual aid and protection are achieved. The cave man fought for existence unaided or even opposed by his fellow man, but today the humblest citizen of our State stands protected by all the power and strength of his Government. Our Government is not the master but the creature of the people. The duty of the State toward the citizens is the duty of the servant to its master. The people have created it; the people, by common consent, permit its continual existence.
>
> One of these duties of the State is that of caring for those of its citizens who find themselves the victims of such adverse circumstances as makes them unable to obtain even the necessities for mere existence without the aid of others. That responsibility is recognized by every civilized Nation.

With a simple and profound question, FDR laid the groundwork in New York State for a vast program of Depression-era relief, a prelude to the New Deal he would introduce after his election to the presidency. By posing a question that forces rethinking the most basic of premises, a leader can guide an entire organization outside the box and toward innovation.

THE UNPRECEDENTED
AND THE UNUSUAL

"I have started out on the tasks that lie ahead by breaking . . . absurd traditions . . ."

—Speech to the 1932 Democratic National Convention, Chicago, July 2, 1932

As former assistant secretary of the navy and an avid skipper of small sailing craft, Franklin Roosevelt cheerfully confessed himself a "good sailor." But he hated to fly. Nevertheless when word came to him in Albany that he had won nomination as the Democratic Party's candidate for president, FDR instantly boarded a plane and flew to Chicago.

He didn't have to. In fact he shouldn't have. In those days nominees never appeared at their party's political convention to make an acceptance speech. Instead, as Roosevelt noted, the candidate was supposed to "remain in professed ignorance of what has happened for weeks until he is formally notified . . . many weeks later." Breaking precedent, Roosevelt appeared before the convention and began by explaining his action:

> The appearance before a national convention of its nominee for president, to be formally notified of his selection, is unprecedented and unusual, but these are

unprecedented and unusual times. I have started out on the tasks that lie ahead by breaking the absurd tradition that the candidate should remain in professed ignorance of what has happened for weeks until he is formally notified of that event many weeks later.

My friends, may this be the symbol of my intention to be honest and to avoid all hypocrisy or sham, to avoid all silly shutting of the eyes to the truth in this campaign. . . .

Let it also be symbolic that in so doing I broke traditions. Let it be from now on the task of our party to break foolish traditions.

"A foolish consistency," Ralph Waldo Emerson wrote, "is the hobgoblin of little minds." The only thing more foolish than adhering to a practice *only* because "that is how it was done before" is to continue such a practice when it no longer makes good sense, when it no longer works, or when unprecedented times and situations call for unprecedented ideas, policies, approaches, and actions.

FDR not only had the courage to break with tradition as necessary but he made certain that those who chose him as their champion, their leader, were made aware that breaking with tradition was his intention. Effective leadership requires effective action, on an immediate, practical level as well as on a symbolic level. It was inconvenient, unpleasant, and—in terms of precedent—unnecessary for FDR to fly to Chicago. As a symbol, however, an overture to a new era—to what he called in this very speech a "New Deal for the American people"—the inconvenient, unpleasant, unprecedented gesture was absolutely necessary. So FDR, who could not walk unaided, took wing.

IF WE MADE IT, WE CAN CHANGE IT

"We must lay hold of the fact that economic laws are not made by nature. They are made by human beings."

—Speech to the 1932 Democratic National Convention, Chicago, July 2, 1932

Addressing the Democratic National Convention in 1932, during the administration of Republican Herbert Hoover, Franklin Roosevelt declared, "Our Republican leaders tell us economic laws— sacred, inviolable, unchangeable—cause panics which no one could prevent." He continued:

> But while they prate of economic laws, men and women are starving. We must lay hold of the fact that economic laws are not made by nature. They are made by human beings.

It often falls to the leader to bring a message of change, but before she can deliver this message, she must first make those she leads aware of the *possibility* of change. Not everything can be changed, but if a thing is made by human beings, human beings can change it. Before bringing to the members of the enterprise the task of change, the leader might well ponder the good sense of the famous Serenity Prayer of Alcoholics Anonymous. "God grant us the serenity to accept things we cannot change, courage to change things we can, and wisdom to know the difference." It is the leader's job to "know the difference," and then it is her job to provide, to shape, and to guide the "courage to change things we can."

REDEFINE THE FAMILIAR

"Every man has a right to life; and this means that he has also a right to make a comfortable living."

> —Speech to the Commonwealth Club of San Francisco,
> September 23, 1932

No American would argue with the assertion of the Declaration of Independence that we all have the inalienable right to "life, liberty, and the pursuit of happiness." No American would argue with the Bill of Rights, which guarantees that no one may be deprived of life, liberty, or property without due process of law. These are basic and very familiar.

And that gets to the heart of Franklin Roosevelt's genius as a leader. He had an unerring instinct for redefining and expanding the familiar to achieve often radical reform. Beginning on the old ground of the right to life, he raised the edifice of the New Deal by extending the definition of that right to encompass a "comfortable living."

In his San Francisco speech, FDR was careful to avoid confusing the right to a comfortable living with a right to live off the government dole. A person may "by sloth or crime decline to exercise that right [to a comfortable living], but," Roosevelt insisted, "it may not be denied him." He pointed out that in the Depression year of 1932, "we have no actual famine or dearth; our industrial and agricultural mechanism can produce enough and to spare." This being the case, "Our government formal and informal, political and economic, owes to every one an avenue to possess himself of a portion of that plenty sufficient for his needs, through his own work."

Under Herbert Hoover, FDR's predecessor and rival in the election of 1932, the federal government played virtually no role in providing direct relief from the Depression. It was not so much that the Hoover administration believed the federal government should not help, but that Hoover and his men were incapable of reimagining the federal government as a body that *could* help. The Hoover administration would agree that everyone has a right to life but that administration would not have accepted the enlargement of that privilege to encompass the right to make a comfortable living. More significantly, it would have been incapable even of imagining such a redefinition. Yet once the redefinition *is* made, the new role for the federal government becomes not only easy to imagine, but inevitable and even incumbent upon that government.

For Roosevelt leadership was not something slapped on top of the old heap that is the status quo. It consisted in questioning and if necessary redefining the status quo. Leadership did not mean pulling the organization along behind the leader but rather growing it in a new way, so that on its own, from its own roots, it could reach whatever height the people imagined for it.

MAKE THE UNFAMILIAR FAMILIAR

"It will succeed if our people understand it . . ."

—Fireside Chat on the National Recovery Administration,
  July 24, 1933

An effective leader learns to understand—and to understand quickly—what most concerns those he leads. Once he understands these concerns, he addresses them, and he bases his actions and policies in large part on them.

In 1933 Roosevelt had a firm grasp on the dominant emotion among the American people: fear. This presented a special leadership dilemma. For FDR proposed to attack the Depression with a dazzling series of innovative and in many cases radical new programs and policies. The new and the unfamiliar are in themselves disturbing, even frightening, to many people. Add this to the fear that already existed, and it looked to be a hard uphill fight to gain acceptance of innovations such as the National Recovery Administration.

Roosevelt's leadership strategy in this Fireside Chat was to overcome the fear of the unfamiliar by doing his best to render the unfamiliar in terms of the familiar. He began with the most basic of concepts: "this simple principle of everybody doing things together." If the new and the unfamiliar were frightening, the related ideas of help, mutual aid, teamwork, cooperation, and pooled strength were very familiar and highly comforting. By "doing things together," FDR explained, "we are starting out on this nationwide attack on unemployment." FDR combined a simple and comforting principle of cooperation in a war against the *real* enemy, the thing everyone fears and has every reason to fear: unemployment.

Having taken the first big step toward dispelling the fog of fear from the idea of the National Recovery Administration, FDR continued very explicitly to emphasize the critical importance of everyone *understanding* what the NRA was all about: "It will succeed if our people understand it—in the big industries, in the little shops, in the great cities, and in the small villages."

Present here are two FDR leadership hallmarks. First, his insistence on full engagement. As a leader FDR understood that he alone could not do all the pulling. Everyone must pull together. The second leadership hallmark is this: inclusiveness—*everyone* must do his or her part, beginning with an effort, at all levels, to understand. The NRA program was not just for big industries or large urban areas, but for everyone at every level.

Having emphasized the critical importance of understanding what the NRA is about, FDR provided assurance that "There is nothing complicated about it . . ." Furthermore, although nothing like the National Recovery Administration had ever before been introduced into American life, "there is nothing particularly new about the principle." The president explained: "It goes back to the basic idea of society and of the nation itself that people acting in a group can accomplish things which no individual acting alone could even hope to bring about."

You cannot get more basic, more elementary than this. While some might choose to see the NRA as a radical new departure from American capitalism—it is, after all, a means of bringing labor, management, and rival firms into close cooperation rather than capitalist competition—FDR explained it as an expression of a timeless and very simple idea, the idea of society and of nationhood, and the very motive that induces people to live and work together rather than separately: "that people acting in a group can accomplish things which no individual acting alone could even hope to bring about." Who could fear this, the very basis of civilization? And who could object to it?

LEAD THE CHANGE

"We have undertaken a new order of things; yet we progress to it under the framework and in the spirit and intent of the American Constitution. . . . We seek [change] through tested liberal traditions, through processes which retain all of the deep essentials of that republican form of representative government first given to a troubled world by the United States."

—Second annual message to Congress, January 4, 1935

Leadership is as much about continuity as it is about change. Facing an economic crisis unprecedented in duration and extent, Roosevelt knew that radical changes in government were called for, yet he also understood that introducing too great a degree of change during a crisis would only tend to deepen the people's sense of crisis. His leadership task became one of defining the necessary change within a familiar framework, namely, the Constitution and "tested liberal traditions."

Leading simultaneously for change and continuity is both critically important and yet a very delicate matter. There is a danger of delivering an ambiguous message or of the leader conveying his own ambivalence. Even worse, there is a danger of delivering a message that simply sounds like double-talk, the worst kind of dishonesty: Here is something entirely new that's worked well in the past!

FDR, however, pulled off the double leadership role precisely by making it clear that the change he proposed not only fitted within the parameters of the Constitution and American tradition but that it grew out of these very things. The validity of the double message depended on having and thoroughly understanding a set of sound principles from which to lead, principles that guided the range of response to events, but that did not destructively limit response. In this sense effective leadership could be understood as the creative and innovative application of tested traditions and commonly valued principles.

LEAD PAST THE FEAR

"I seek reenactment of the historic and traditional American policy which . . . has served us well from the very beginning of our constitutional existence."

> —Message to Congress urging repeal of the embargo provisions of the Neutrality Act of 1937, September 21, 1939

Anxious to stay out of another "European war," the U.S. Congress passed a series of neutrality acts, beginning in August 1935, when Mussolini's Italy invaded Ethiopia. The 1935 act empowered the president to embargo arms shipments to belligerents, and a second act, passed in February 1936, added a prohibition on extending loans or credits to belligerents. Neither of these acts distinguished between aggressor and victim. After the 1936 act expired in 1937, a new act was even more stringent: the United States was not only barred from arming belligerents, but the president could also expand the embargo list to include "strategic materials" (for example, steel). The 1937 act also prohibited U.S. nationals from traveling aboard ships of belligerents; after all, America's entry into World War I had come about in part because German U-boats torpedoed and sank British passenger liners on which Americans traveled and died.

The Nazi invasion of Poland on September 1, 1939, served finally to persuade Roosevelt of what he had long felt: Absolute neutrality had ceased to be in the best interest of the United States. As it became clear to FDR that the United States would almost certainly soon enter the war on the side of Britain and the other Allies, the Neutrality Act of 1937 was clearly too constraining. We needed *now* to help the nations at whose side we would *soon* fight. So FDR addressed Congress on repealing the embargo provisions of the 1937 neutrality act.

While he was persuaded of the urgency of ending the embargo, he also understood that this would be a frightening step for lawmakers as well as the American people. As always, his first objective was to address the fear and overcome it. He did so by presenting this bold action not as a new step, fraught with risk, but as a return to the normal and traditional state of things: "I seek a greater consistency through the repeal of the embargo provisions, and a return to international law." He underscored the word *return* with the word *reenactment* and with the words *historic* and *traditional:*

> I seek reenactment of the historic and traditional American policy which, except for the disastrous interlude of the Embargo and Non-Intercourse Acts [in the period just prior to the War of 1812], has served us well from the very beginning of our constitutional existence.

In the end Congress did not repeal the embargo but instead replaced the entire 1937 act with the Neutrality Act of 1939, which essentially recapitulated the earlier act with the important exception of allowing cash-and-carry sales of arms and strategic materials to belligerents except as might be prohibited by presidential proclamation. This was, in fact, a substantial step away from neutrality. By international law and custom, neutral nations are permitted to trade, even in arms, with all other nations and are deemed to remain neutral as long as no belligerent is explicitly excluded from such trade. While the 1939 act permitted arms trade with all belligerents, it also provided for exclusion of trade with any belligerents the president might specify.

"I seek reenactment of the historic and traditional American policy which . . . has served us well from the very beginning of our constitutional existence." It is a platitude to observe that the future is built on the past, but it is nevertheless effective in persuasive communication to predicate the present and future tenses on the past tense. In essence FDR declared: *I seek* (present tense) *what has served us well*—which is not just past tense, but the past perfect tense, the tense reserved for expressing accomplished facts.

There is no deception in this communication. FDR was not trying to make a new step, a step into the unknown, look like an step back into the familiar and safe past. But instead of emphasizing the aspects of novelty and uncertainty, he tempered these with the context of history, tradition, and proven policy. In leadership communication as much depends on the perspective and perception that are created as on the facts that are presented. The frame is as important as the picture it contains.

ON MOTIVATION

PRESENT A CHOICE

". . . we must either shut our eyes . . . or, we must open our eyes . . ."

> —Acceptance speech for vice presidential nomination,
> August 9, 1920

In 1920 Franklin Roosevelt accepted nomination as running mate to James M. Cox of Ohio, the presidential candidate up against Republican Warren G. Harding. A realist, FDR knew that in the post–World War I national climate of isolationism, the voters would almost certainly reject the Democratic stance of international engagement, the position of outgoing war president Woodrow Wilson, and embrace instead the isolationism proposed by the Republicans. Whereas Wilson had championed the League of Nations, Harding summed up the Republican attitude toward it with a simple statement: "The League is not for us."

Yet FDR ran and he ran as he would always run, with buoyant confidence and an energetic determination to get his message across. He boiled down the great issue of the campaign to a choice:

> In our world problems, we must either shut our eyes,
> sell our newly built merchant marine to more far-seeing
> foreign powers, crush utterly by embargo and harass-

149

ing legislation our foreign trade, close our ports, build an impregnable wall of costly armaments and live, as the Orient used to live, a hermit nation, dreaming of the past, or, we must open our eyes and see that modern civilization has become so complex and the lives of civilized men so interwoven with the lives of other men in other countries as to make it impossible to be in this world and not of it. We must see that it is impossible to avoid, except by monastic seclusion, those honorable and intimate foreign relations which the fearful hearted shudderingly miscall by that Devil's catch word "international complications."

Either/or—this *or* that—is a powerful leadership tool. Persuasive communication invariably leads to action, and the readiest way to lead people to action is to present them with a choice.

Delivering a choice, presenting an *either* and an *or,* is bold leadership. It is also high-stakes leadership, because it runs the risk of oversimplification or of outright distortion. An either/or presentation may simply put the organization on the horns of a dilemma—a most uncomfortable place to be. Instead of inciting the desired action, two other outcomes are possible: First, given the choice, the group may choose the "wrong" alternative—that is, the alternative the leader does not want chosen. Or second, the group may simply refuse to be seated on the horns of that dilemma. It may reject both choices and select yet a third alternative.

An effective leader looks for opportunities to present clear, even stark choices. But she always remains wary of the dangers of oversimplification, distortion, and a failure to calculate all of the alternatives.

POINT A FINGER

"The answer is not hard to find."

—Second gubernatorial inaugural address, Albany,
January 1, 1931

In his second inaugural address as governor of New York, delivered on January 1, 1931, FDR asked a question: "But why are our local governments archaic in design, unsuited for the purpose for which they are established, unsatisfactory in their functioning, and profligate in the spending of taxpayers' contributions?" And he answered it:

> The answer is not hard to find. It is because the individual citizen is indifferent to his local government problems. The stress of business competition in this hectic twentieth century of ours, the even more feverish pursuit of pleasure to compensate for our strenuous business days—these so occupy the time and thought of our average taxpayer as to leave no inclination either to study or assist in the conduct of the community in which he lives. We do not trust our personal business affairs to strangers; we do not take our pleasures vicar-

iously; but when it comes to running our local communities we gladly let John Doe do it.

An effective leader never regards those he leads as passive pawns and ciphers, mere followers. More important, he never permits them to think of themselves in this way. FDR pointed out a problem that many of his constituents regularly complained about: the inadequacy and inefficiency of local government. He agreed that this was a problem, and then he deftly pointed a finger at the source of the problem—his audience, the very people he had been elected to lead.

Often a leader is faced with the task of getting his people involved, of getting them engaged with an issue or a problem. When others point fingers in every direction, it may fall to the leader to point back. In doing this, there is always the risk of alienating those you lead. After all nobody likes being blamed. FDR managed this risk by providing his listeners with an explanation of their indifference "to local government problems." They were too busy, either with business or, understandably, with pleasure. This was presented not as an excuse for indifference, but as a reason, an explanation. Nor did FDR leave the situation at that. His purpose was not merely to identify the source of a problem, to analyze its cause, and then to allow people to nod their heads in agreement. Effective leadership communication always moves people to action or at least in the direction of action. Having provided an explanation for indifference, FDR continued by pointing out that "We do not trust our personal business affairs to strangers; we do not take our pleasures vicariously." Yet, he continued, we do something very much like this when it comes to local government.

The conclusion was inescapable. What's unacceptable in private life should be regarded as even less acceptable in the life of the community. The solution—the course of action—was clear:

Transform local government by becoming involved in it, under-standing it, and participating in it. A highly effective leader, FDR invited self-examination, but he did not leave his audience sus-pended in idle introspection. He pointed to an end and purpose of this self-examination: appropriate action.

BUILD FROM BOTTOM TO TOP

"It was a great plan because it was built from bottom to top and not from top to bottom."

—Radio address on the national economic emergency, April 7, 1932

On April 7, 1932, before he had even been chosen as the Democratic candidate for president of the United States, New York governor Roosevelt addressed the nation over the radio. His subject was the Depression, the national economic emergency.

An effective leader—one who makes policy and who then persuades others to embrace that policy—must be like the Roman god Janus, equipped with two faces, two sets of eyes, one always looking forward and the other looking back. A leader has to face the future, but with a knowledge of the past. She must evaluate the present and future in terms of experience, yet without letting past experience retard or discourage innovation. Finally, an effective leader understands that precedent is always a powerful persuader. People embrace the familiar, even when they must be led toward something new.

Thus in approaching the subject of the Great Depression, a national economic emergency of *unprecedented* scale, FDR began with reference to another "great national emergency, the [First] World War":

> Success then was due to a leadership whose vision carried beyond the timorous and futile gesture of sending a tiny army of 150,000 trained soldiers and the regular navy to the aid of our allies. The generalship of that moment conceived of a whole nation mobilized for war: economic, industrial, social, and military resources gathered into a vast unit capable of and actually in the process of throwing into the scales 10 million men equipped with physical needs and sustained by the realization that behind them were the united efforts of 110 million human beings. It was a great plan because it was built from bottom to top and not from top to bottom.

The Great War was a great national emergency, but also a great national triumph. Why? Because of leadership with vision, specifically the vision of each and every American mobilized for the war effort, united in that endeavor, but also each aware of his or her individual responsibility within that united effort. For FDR this was the essence of leadership: an ability to conceive and direct united effort without ever losing sight of the fact that such effort is the sum of well-motivated individual efforts. An effective leader must give those he leads a vision of the whole—the big picture—yet he must never allow anyone to believe that he or she is not absolutely essential to that big picture.

E pluribus unum is the Latin motto on the Great Seal of the United States: *From many, one.* Leadership in a democracy recognizes that one must lead both the "many" and the "one," and that this must be done with perfect simultaneity. Thus leadership plans need to be built from the bottom to the top. They cannot start at the top and work down, but neither can they start and stop at the bottom. The effective leader plans for each individual as well as for the entire enterprise. Any plan that focuses on the one at the expense of the other must be rejected. From the perspective of any individual, an effective leader comes across as speaking directly to him or her while also addressing the collective enterprise.

REPORT

"I come . . . to give you my report . . . to tell you about what we have been doing and what we are planning to do."

—Fireside Chat on new economic policies, May 7, 1933

Few people will come out and say that communication is a bad thing, but many bosses, managers, executives, and other leaders really do believe that too much communication invites discontent, dispute, and second-guessing. It undermines discipline, they think. It dilutes power and authority. Such leaders see the members of their enterprise in the same light as the British soldiers in "The Charge of the Light Brigade" saw themselves: "Ours not to reason why, / Ours but to do and die." It is, of course, well to remember that Tennyson's poem commemorates a spectacular military blunder in the Crimean War, a military enterprise that consisted of little other than blunders and the blind obedience of officers and men who knew they were being ordered, by mistake, into collective suicide but without question followed orders nevertheless.

Can this really be a good thing?

Certainly FDR didn't think so. His leadership style was founded on sharing information and explaining, on the basis of that shared information, whatever decisions had been made and actions taken. People may be coerced into compliance and obedience, it is true, but how much more effective it is to give people the opportunity to buy into a course of action, a policy, a program, to buy into it of their own free will. Given the depths of the crisis of 1933, Roosevelt did not want obedience or even compliance, he wanted an embrace, enthusiastic, spontaneous, and born of a full understanding of what was at stake. Motivation addresses the whole person and requires understanding from the person you wish to motivate—the more thorough the better. Hide nothing, report everything, explain everything: what you have been doing, what you are planning to do.

WHERE THERE'S A WILL

"They will if they want to."

—Fireside Chat on the National Recovery Administration,
July 24, 1933

A well-chosen, good-humored anecdote can do more than lighten
the tone of a talk on a serious subject. It can make that subject
more human, more approachable, and more clear. FDR sum-
moned up a recollection concerning an admired American, a past
president and a folk hero:

> When Andrew Jackson, "Old Hickory," died, someone
> asked, "Will he go to heaven?" and the answer was,
> "He will if he wants to." If I am asked whether the
> American people will pull themselves out of this de-
> pression, I answer, "They will if they want to."

The message here was subtly threefold:

First and foremost, Roosevelt underscored that it wouldn't be
the "government" or the "economy" that would end the Depression, but the "American people," who had to "pull themselves out
of this Depression." FDR always presented himself as a leader, not

a king or a god. Guidance and policy he could provide; the rest had to come from the people.

Second, FDR implied that the people would succeed only *if* they truly wanted success. The desire and willingness to make sacrifices and to accept new ideas had to be present and had to come from within the group.

Third, by comparing the American people of 1933 to "Old Hickory," a man celebrated for his toughness, his courage, and above all, his indomitable will, FDR powerfully expressed his confidence that Americans did not lack the will to pull themselves out of the Depression.

An effective leader sets goals, points a path toward those goals, and supplies the means for reaching them. The required will, however, the necessary effort, must ultimately come from those who are led.

REQUIRE IMPROVEMENT

"I am not satisfied with the progress thus far made."

—Eighth annual message to Congress, January 6, 1941

As has been observed elsewhere, an effective leader is, in part, a combination cheerleader and monitor of progress. At the brink of World War II, the U.S. Army was not a third-rate force, but a fifteenth-rate force, at about 250,000 men, ranking behind fourteenth-rated Romania in strength. FDR and Congress embarked on a crash program of military expansion, and on January 6, 1941, the president reported to Congress: "The army and navy—have made substantial progress during the past year." Moreover, "Actual experience is improving and speeding up our methods of [war materials] production with every passing day."

Then FDR continued: "And today's best is not good enough for tomorrow. I am not satisfied with the progress thus far made."

So much for the cheerleading. Roosevelt acknowledged progress—ongoing progress—but he wanted above all to avoid the great enemy of any dynamic organization, complacency. It is a startling and powerful thing when the leader tells you, point-blank, "I am not satisfied." Depending on the leader's next words, you can either write off this dissatisfaction to the personality of the leader ("He's *never* satisfied") or you can take the remark as a call to action. FDR chose his next words carefully: "The men in charge of the program represent the best in training, in ability, and in patriotism. They are not satisfied with the progress thus far made." So much for being able to write this off to the attitude of an individual; FDR presented his view as that of the consensus of those who were in a position to know best. Then he concluded with the true criterion of "progress" in preparedness for war: "None of us will be satisfied until the job is done."

From this point on in his speech, FDR broadly outlined a program for accelerating progress. Just as he was careful not to overlook or deny the progress that had been made, he avoided merely expressing dissatisfaction with results thus far, but instead pointed the way toward fully satisfactory progress. An effective leader is never hesitant to express his opinion, his evaluation of the situation, but he always takes care to acknowledge effort and achievement, to avert complacency in doing so, and to deliver only creative criticism, which at the very least specifies a direction toward improvement. To do less than this is to alienate the leader from the group and the group from the leader.

GET INTERACTIVE

"Look at your map."

—Fireside Chat on the war, February 23, 1942

From the beginning of the war, especially during those early days when the news was so grim, Franklin Roosevelt believed it to be critically important that every American understand the war and the war effort. Because it was a global war, fought in places wholly unfamiliar to most Americans, FDR took the unusual step of asking, in advance of this Fireside Chat, that people obtain a "map of the whole earth," so that they could "follow with me in the references which I shall make to the world-encircling battle lines of this war." It was reported that sales of maps and atlases skyrocketed just prior to the announced February 23, 1942, broadcast. Clearly FDR had gotten the people involved.

He put this interactive approach to dramatic good use. If possible, read these few paragraphs with a world map in front of *you:*

> Look at your map. Look at the vast area of China, with its millions of fighting men. Look at the vast area of Russia, with its powerful armies and proven military might. Look at the British Isles, Australia, New Zealand, the Dutch Indies, India, the Near East and the Conti-

nent of Africa, with their sources of raw materials—
their resources of raw materials, and of peoples determined to resist Axis domination. Look too at North
America, Central America and South America. It is obvious what would happen if all of these great reservoirs
of power were cut off from each other either by enemy
action or by self-imposed isolation:

1. First, in such a case, we could no longer send aid of
   any kind to China—to the brave people who, for
   nearly five years, have withstood Japanese assault,
   destroyed hundreds of thousands of Japanese soldiers and vast quantities of Japanese war munitions.
   It is essential that we help China in her magnificent
   defense and in her inevitable counteroffensive—for
   that is one important element in the ultimate defeat
   of Japan.

2. Secondly, if we lost communication with the southwest Pacific, all of that area, including Australia and
   New Zealand and the Dutch Indies, would fall under Japanese domination. Japan in such a case could
   release great numbers of ships and men to launch
   attacks on a large scale against the coasts of the
   Western Hemisphere—South America and Central
   America, and North America—including Alaska.
   At the same time, she could immediately extend
   her conquests in the other direction toward India,
   through the Indian Ocean, to Africa, to the Near
   East and try to join forces with Germany and Italy.

3. Third, if we were to stop sending munitions to the
   British and the Russians in the Mediterranean area,
   in the Persian Gulf and the Red Sea, we would be
   helping the Nazis to overrun Turkey, and Syria, and
   Iraq, and Persia—that is now called Iran—Egypt

and the Suez Canal, the whole coast of North Africa itself and with that inevitably the whole coast of West Africa—putting Germany within easy striking distance of South America—fifteen hundred miles away.

4. Fourth, if by such a fatuous policy, we ceased to protect the North Atlantic supply line to Britain and to Russia, we would help to cripple the splendid counteroffensive by Russia against the Nazis, and we should help to deprive Britain of essential food supplies and munitions.

The president continued in this vein, guiding his listeners through the war with the aid of their maps. "This is war," he said, and he wanted everyone to understand it, individually and thoroughly. *This* is war—and *that* is motivation.

THAT SUBTLE WEAPON

". . . there is [a] subtle weapon that, more than anything else, spells victory or defeat. That weapon is morale—the morale of a people who know they are fighting 'the good fight.'"

—Radio address on the annual appeal for the National Foundation for Infantile Paralysis, January 29, 1944

No one would deny the importance of morale, and yet too often many of us treat it as a frill, an adjunct, or extra, that is added on after all of the "real"—that is, physical or financial—needs are taken care of.

It is true that morale alone cannot get the job done. Planning, equipment, intelligence, finance: typically many things must be put into place before success can be achieved. But at the very least, morale provides the leverage that multiplies the effectiveness of whatever other elements are necessary to achieving the organization's goals. More often, morale acts as a catalyst, the very ingredient absolutely necessary to putting those other elements into action.

Whatever the precise role morale serves in a given enterprise, it is not sufficient to include it as an afterthought. An effective leader makes the issue of morale central to every endeavor of the group.

YOU KNOW WHO YOU ARE

"There are still many people in the United States who have not bought War Bonds, or who have not bought as many as they can afford. Everyone knows for himself whether he falls into that category or not. In some cases his neighbors know too."

—Fireside Chat on the fifth war loan drive, June 12, 1944

Shortly after the Allied landings at Normandy on D-Day, President Roosevelt made an appeal on behalf of the fifth war loan, a major war bond drive. After observing that "Americans have all worked together to make this day"—D-Day—"possible," he reminded his listeners that there were still people who had not purchased bonds or who had not purchased as many as they could afford. "Everyone knows for himself whether he falls into that category or not." Few appeals are stronger than an appeal to conscience. Yet with a wry twist of the knife, FDR added: "In some cases his neighbors know too."

Direction and motivation that come from within are always more powerful than compulsion from without. A wise leader makes his first appeal to conscience and only afterward to forces outside of conscience.

SHARE THE LESSON

"I remember that my old schoolmaster, Dr. Peabody, said . . ."

—Fourth inaugural address, January 20, 1945

Many leaders back away from the challenge of providing inspiration. They feel inadequate to the task of creating genuine spirit, having lived ordinary lives among ordinary people. They have no stock of famous names and great words on which to draw. They ask, in all humility: *Who am I to inspire anyone?*

But no leader can afford to shirk the responsibility of inspiring the enterprise. It is part and parcel of leadership.

Inspiration does not require personal greatness or a life of noble deeds among celebrated men and women. Each of us can recall some life experience, however homely, however ordinary, that guided and inspired us. Of all the great men and women Franklin Roosevelt knew and worked with during his life and career, he chose, on the occasion of his fourth inaugural address, to recall the words not of a statesman or political leader, but of his "old schoolmaster" at the Groton School, Endicott Peabody:

> Things in life will not always run smoothly. Sometimes we will be rising toward the heights—then all will seem to reverse itself and start downward. The great

fact to remember is that the trend of civilization is forever upward; that a line drawn through the middle of the peaks and the valleys of centuries always has an upward trend.

FDR might have called on some more public voice for words of wisdom and inspiration: the Bible, Plato, Washington, Jefferson, Lincoln, or perhaps a statesman or philosopher of the present day. Instead he reached into his own past and found words spoken by an obscure schoolmaster. But they were words that meant something to him, words he felt deeply, and words he remembered through the passing decades. So he shared them in the confidence that because they had meaning for him, they would have meaning for others.

That is the sovereign standard by which to judge the inspirational value of whatever you have to say. The words need not come from some high and mighty source. But they must come from a source that has meaning for you. You are not so very different from those you are expected to inspire and lead. What is valuable to you, therefore, will surely offer value to others. Share that value.

ON MAKING
EVERYONE COUNT

INTERDEPENDENCE

"No nation can long endure half bankrupt."

—Radio address on the national economic emergency,
April 7, 1932

Leadership of any complex enterprise is rarely a matter of convincing people to "follow me," but rather a mission to persuade each individual member of the enterprise that he or she has common cause with every other member. This is an especially difficult mission when times are tough and *individual* survival looms larger than the survival of the collective enterprise.

Whatever else they may be, human beings are biological creatures, charged, as all such creatures are, with an instinct for self-preservation. Thus at the onset of the Great Depression, the human instinct of the American people—or of each American person—was to save his or her own skin. Urbanites, for example, desperately clinging to their jobs, felt they could not afford—quite literally, could not afford—to care for the farmers, who had been hit first and hardest by the hard times. In his April 7, 1932, radio address on the national economic emergency, FDR called these people "shallow thinkers" and explained that they failed to realize . . . that approximately one-half of our whole population, fifty or sixty million people, earn their living by farming or in small towns whose existence immediately depends on farms. They have today lost their purchasing power. Why? They are receiving for farm products less than the cost to them of growing these farm products. The result of this loss of purchasing power is that many other millions of people engaged in industry in the cities cannot sell industrial products to the farming half of the nation. This brings home to every city worker that his own employment is directly tied up with the farmer's dollar. No nation can long endure half bankrupt. Main Street, Broadway, the mills, the mines will close if half the buyers are broke.

FDR's immediate point was "the conclusion that one of the essential parts of a national program of restoration must be to restore purchasing power to the farming half of the country. Without this the wheels of railroads and of factories will not turn." But his greater point was that we of this enterprise called America were all interdependent. He did not express this with a pronouncement of abstract piety or even of poetry—say John Donne's declaration that "no man is an island"—but as a straightforward, irrefutable fact of economics.

That this issue of interdependence can be expressed in dollars and cents does not diminish it as a moral and ethical statement. As a leader, one of the insights to which FDR inevitably led people is the remarkable revelation that the apparent gap between profit and ethics, between the ideal and the practical, is just that: apparent. In reality, charity or taxation to support others is not an *idealistic* sacrifice, but a *practical* means to profit. The "shallow thinkers" notwithstanding, the hard, real, practical, and inescapable truth is that we're all in this together: a team.

REMEMBER THE FORGOTTEN

"Let us look a little at the recent history and the simple economics, the kind of economics that you and I and the average man and woman talk."

—Speech to the 1932 Democratic National Convention, Chicago, July 2, 1932

The Great Depression. Even today, what best captures that hard era are certain photographic images, the work of Dorothea Lange, for example, focusing on migrant farm families caught in the Dust Bowl, or Walker Evans's images of urban unemployed men, idle men, desperate men. Such images, although varied, made in different American towns, cities, and villages, depicting a vast gallery of faces, have a compelling sameness to them: They all portray what the people of the Depression called the "forgotten man."

FDR approached leadership with the conviction that no leader can afford to forget anyone. And he addressed the plight of the "forgotten man" head on.

The first step toward recalling the forgotten and including the excluded is to be certain that you understand the issues that bear most directly on these "forgotten" lives. Good leaders always take this step. Great leaders step beyond it, articulating and explaining those issues more clearly, fully, and deeply than even those who are most affected by them can. "Let us look a little at the recent history and the simple economics," Roosevelt invited his Democratic Party convention audience, "the kind of economics that you and I and the average man and woman talk."

He began, then, by gathering everyone together: you, me, the average man, the average woman. The implied promise was clear: no one will be forgotten.

> In the years before 1929 we know that this country had completed a vast cycle of building and inflation; for ten years we expanded on the theory of repairing the wastes of the war, but actually expanding far beyond that, and also beyond our natural and normal growth. Now it is worth remembering, and the cold figures of finance prove it, that during that time there was little or no drop in the prices that the consumer had to pay, although those same figures proved that the cost of production fell very greatly; corporate profit resulting from this period was enormous; at the same time little of that profit was devoted to the reduction of prices. The consumer was forgotten. Very little of it went into increased wages; the worker was forgotten, and by no means an adequate proportion was even paid out in dividends—the stockholder was forgotten.

Roosevelt explained why the "forgotten man" was forgotten. But he did much more. Who is the forgotten man? The migrant in the photo by Lange? The idled laborer in the Walker Evans composition? Yes—but also the consumer, the worker, *and* the stockholder. In short, everyone (save the corporations themselves) became forgotten men and women. At the heart of every FDR leadership message was this: We are all in it together, for better or worse, for richer or poorer, in sickness and in health. And that included the government: "And, incidentally," FDR continued, "very little of it [corporate profit] was taken by taxation to the beneficent government of those [pre-Depression] years."

Having described the situation leading up to the economic crash of 1929, FDR asked "What was the result?"

> Enormous corporate surpluses piled up—the most stupendous in history. Where, under the spell of delirious speculation, did those surpluses go? Let us talk economics that the figures prove and that we can understand. Why, they went chiefly in two directions: first, into new and unnecessary plants which now stand stark and idle; and second, into the call-money market of Wall Street, either directly by the corporations, or indirectly through the banks. Those are the facts. Why blink at them?

This was a speech no presidential nominee had ever made before because, adhering to outworn tradition, no nominee ever appeared before a national convention to accept, personally, the nomination of his party. Breaking what he called this "absurd" tradition, the fiction that the "candidate should remain in professed ignorance of what has happened for weeks until he is formally notified," FDR declared that his precedent-shattering appearance before the convention was a "symbol of my intention to be honest and avoid all hypocrisy." And so in his exposition of the "facts" of the Great Depression, he asked, "Why blink at them?" A leader faces the truth and, equally important, leads others to face it as well.

"Then came the crash," FDR continued. "You know the story."

> Surpluses invested in unnecessary plants became idle. Men lost their jobs; purchasing power dried up; banks became frightened and started calling loans. Those

who had money were afraid to part with it. Credit contracted. Industry stopped. Commerce declined, and unemployment mounted.

And there we are today.

Picture again, for a moment, those faces in the great photographs of the Depression era. They are faces of poverty, they are weathered faces, they are faces worn by care, but most of all, they are bewildered, anxious faces. To the common man, the "forgotten man," the Great Depression came like a plague of the Dark Ages, a great malevolent force seemingly beyond any human control and certainly beyond the control of any individual farmer, laborer, or even stockholder. The results of the Depression were all too clear—hunger and homelessness—but the nature of it was, to most, mysterious and, therefore, all the more terrifying. FDR's speech aims at taking out some of the terror. It presents a compelling, brief analysis of the Great Depression in language that forgets no one, that everyone can understand. It does not soften the truth, turn from it, blink at it, but faces the truth squarely and leads all who listen to do the same.

In crisis many are forgotten. Leadership in crisis requires that no one be forgotten. In crisis not only are many people forgotten, but the truth itself may also escape. A leader, in crisis above all other times, does not blink at facts and never forgets the truth.

THE LEADERSHIP EQUATION

"It is your problem no less than it is mine. Together we cannot fail."

—Fireside Chat on the banking crisis, March 12, 1933

All effective leaders pay close attention to pronouns. They recognize that the ideal leadership communication transforms *I* and *you* into *we*. Call it the leadership equation.

FDR concluded his Fireside Chat on the banking crisis by both taking ownership of the banking problem *and* by sharing it: "It is your problem no less than it is mine." The "your" and "mine" are precisely equivalent in this formulation, and they create a mighty rhetorical springboard for the president to jump to this assertion: "Together we cannot fail."

The epidemic of bank failures that swept the United States during February and early March 1933 created a nationwide panic born of a feeling of helplessness. Most people thought: *The government has to do something. I can't do everything.* FDR's Fireside Chat explained what the government did indeed do but, even more important, the chat empowered listeners, so that they no longer needed to believe themselves helpless. Not only *could* they do something positive in this crisis, the successful resolution of the crisis *required* them to pitch in by acting calmly, patiently, and with confidence.

WHOLE LEADERSHIP

"If all of our people have work and fair wages and fair profits, they can buy the products of their neighbors, and business is good. But if you take away the wages and the profits of half of them, business is only half as good. It does not help much if the fortunate half is very prosperous; the best way is for everybody to be reasonably prosperous."

—Fireside Chat on the National Recovery Administration, July 24, 1933

In Oliver Stone's popular 1987 film *Wall Street,* the archetypal corporate raider Gordon Gecko proclaimed—to a round of applause—that "Greed is good." Greed, he argued, is the great motivator and engine of achievement.

And nobody disagreed in the movie. FDR, however, devoted much of his leadership effort to countering this very position. The problem with greed is that it produces nothing but one-sided deals. The ultimate expression of greed is theft, and the problem with theft is that it is a dead end. You cannot keep stealing from the same person again and again. At some point, he will stop you—or if he does not, he will run out of things you can steal.

Confronting the Great Depression, FDR saw as his first and most pressing goal the establishment of emergency measures "to reestablish credit and to head people in the opposite direction by preventing distress and providing as much work as possible through governmental agencies." Such steps, Roosevelt told his radio audience in his Fireside Chat on the National Recovery Administration, were "foundation stones." Now, he said:

> Now I come to the links which will build us a more lasting prosperity. I have said that we cannot attain that in a nation half boom and half broke. If all of our people have work and fair wages and fair profits, they can buy the products of their neighbors, and business is good. But if you take away the wages and the profits of half of them, business is only half as good. It does not help much if the fortunate half is very prosperous; the best way is for everybody to be reasonably prosperous.

FDR's great leadership project, during the Depression, was to transform the half-picture most individuals have into the whole picture. If you have something to sell, you need someone with the ability to buy. To obtain the wherewithal to buy, you must have something to sell, along with a buyer for that thing. Greed looks at only one side of this inevitable and immutable equation. Greed is hard enough to overcome during the best of times. During the worst of times, greed *seems* to promise the best chance for survival. Roosevelt needed people to look beyond this fear-induced vision.

He led the American people to wider vistas in part through his speeches and Fireside Chats, but he did not depend on words alone. FDR's New Deal brought a dazzling succession of innovative government programs, most of which were aimed at managing greed and creating a nation in which "everybody" could be "reasonably prosperous." The subject of this July 24, 1933 Fireside Chat was one of the most important pieces of New Deal legislation, the National Industrial Recovery Act of 1933. Enacted at

the urging of FDR, it was an emergency measure intended to fos-
ter industrial recovery and help combat widespread unemployment by calling for industrial self-regulation, which included the
drafting of codes of fair competition for the protection of employers as well as consumers and competitors. These codes, to be
drawn up by industry, would be subject to public hearings. The
administration was authorized to intervene in helping management and labor conclude voluntary agreements dealing with hours
of work, rates of pay, and the fixing of prices. Employees were
given the right to organize and bargain collectively and could not
be required, as a condition of employment, to join or to refrain
from joining a labor organization. By separate executive order the
National Recovery Administration (NRA) was put into operation
to administer the act. It was a bold experiment in managing collective human motivation, sentiment, and behavior. FDR, determined to make the NRA work, delivered his Fireside Chat to
explain it as a means of making the nation, in every sense of the
word, whole again.

SMASH CYNICISM

"It is time to provide a smashing answer for those cynical men who say that a democracy cannot be honest and efficient."

—Fireside Chat on the Works Relief Program, April 28, 1935

Ralph Waldo Emerson once observed that "Nothing great is accomplished without enthusiasm." We might add a sentence to that: "And nothing at all is accomplished with cynicism." Cynicism is the great bane of all leaders, because it is not only the negation of hope and confidence, but of possibility itself. FDR confronted it head-on in explaining to the American people how the Works Relief Program, a great federal public works enterprise designed to provide employment for millions by creating many useful projects for the nation, would function.

He began by appealing for creative criticism as a "smashing answer" to the cynics:

> It is time to provide a smashing answer for those cynical men who say that a democracy cannot be honest and efficient. If you will help, this can be done. I, therefore, hope you will watch the work in every corner of this nation. Feel free to criticize. Tell me of instances where work can be done better, or where

improper practices prevail. Neither you nor I want criticism conceived in a purely fault-finding or partisan spirit, but I am jealous of the right of every citizen to call to the attention of his or her government examples of how the public money can be more effectively spent for the benefit of the American people.

FDR did not ask for yes-men and cheerleaders. He asked for critics—creative, engaged, committed critics; not the cynic, who is disengaged, uncommitted, and anything but creative. Indeed while the cynic criticizes, he is in reality no true critic at all, because as a cheerleader is uncritical in dispensing approval, a cynic is uncritical in finding fault. To him *everything* looks uniformly bad.

The effective leader understands that the opposite of cynicism is not mindless enthusiasm, but thoughtful enthusiasm: a sufficiently high degree of commitment to the enterprise to motivate informed, constructive, creative criticism.

MIRROR THE ACHIEVEMENT

"This morning I came, I saw, and I was conquered, as everyone would be who sees for the first time this great feat of mankind."

—Speech at Boulder Dam, September 30, 1935

Boulder Dam, renamed Hoover Dam by Congress in 1947, is one of the greatest engineering and construction projects humankind ever attempted. Located in Black Canyon on the Colorado River, about thirty miles southeast of Las Vegas, Nevada, Hoover Dam is 726.4 feet from foundation rock to the roadway on the crest of the dam. If you could weigh it, you'd find it tipped the scales at 6,600,000 tons—the weight of 4,360,000 cubic yards of concrete, enough material to build a monument one hundred feet square and 2.5 miles high or to pave a standard two-lane highway, sixteen feet wide, from San Francisco to New York City. The dam's purpose is to control flooding and provide irrigation and other water needs for a seven-state area, and to generate electricity for a large portion of the Southwest. The Boulder Canyon Project Act was declared effective on June 25, 1929, on the eve of the Depression (during the administration of President Herbert Hoover), and contracts for construction were let in 1931, when the Depression was well under way. The mighty Colorado River was diverted around the dam site on November 14, 1932, and the first concrete was poured on June 6, 1933. On February 1, 1935, the dam began impounding water in the lake it would create, Lake Mead. The last concrete was poured on May 29, and President Roosevelt dedicated the dam on September 30.

What is the role of a leader in celebrating great collective achievement? It is first and foremost giving credit where credit is most due: "Senator Pittman," FDR began his speech, "Secretary Ickes, Governors of the Colorado's States, and You Especially Who Have Built Boulder Dam . . ."

And next, it is to mirror the achievement, to reveal, to throw into vivid relief just what it is that has been done:

> Ten years ago the place where we are gathered was an unpeopled, forbidding desert. In the bottom of a gloomy canyon, whose precipitous walls rose to a height of more than a thousand feet, flowed a turbulent, dangerous river. The mountains on either side of the canyon were difficult of access with neither road nor trail, and their rocks were protected by neither trees nor grass from the blazing heat of the sun. The site of Boulder City was a cactus-covered waste. The transformation wrought here in these years is a twentieth-century marvel.

Transformation is the key word, the transformation of waste into productivity, of danger into safety, of the wild forces of nature into energy useful for humankind. Such a transformation would have been a marvel at any time and in any place, but in the depths of Depression-burdened America, the transformation took on an even greater importance. On the most immediate, literal level, FDR pointed to the achievement of Boulder Dam as an example of "the thousands of projects undertaken by the federal government, by the states, and by the counties and municipalities in recent years." The dam would not only prevent floods, provide water, and generate electricity, transforming a wasteland into a wonderland, it would provide—and would continue to provide—employment for thousands.

FDR wanted the American people to see the dam as a spectacular product of the New Deal but on a more idealistic level, he pointed to the great dam as a product of the undaunted spirit of America. Afflicted by unremitting drought and ruthless Depression, American know-how, will, and government—as FDR said, "American resourcefulness, American skill and determination"—created a working, productive monument that would be titanic in any age and under any set of economic circumstances.

As Roosevelt saw it, Boulder Dam was a great and complex project that conveyed a great and simple message: What we can dream, we can do. And the proof was that we had done it.

WE ARE ALL IN IT

"We must share together the bad news and the good news, the defeats and the victories—the changing fortunes of war."

—Fireside Chat on war with Japan, December 9, 1941

Leaders direct shared effort. This means that everyone shares in the benefits of the enterprise and also in its liabilities and griefs. FDR excelled at bringing people together: "We are now in this war. We are all in it—all the way. Every single man, woman, and child is a partner in the most tremendous undertaking of our American history." As terrible as the prospect of war is, by presenting it as a united, all-out effort in the "the most tremendous undertaking of our American history," Roosevelt made it sound almost exciting. Indeed talk to anyone who lived through World War II and you cannot mistake the sense of having been part of something truly significant—not just a grim necessity, but with all of its pain and sacrifice, a collectively enriching experience.

But FDR continued: "We must share together the bad news and the good news, the defeats and the victories—the changing fortunes of war." And: "So far, the news has been all bad."

Roosevelt did not turn away from this bad news and he did not ask the people of America to turn away, either. On the contrary, he detailed it, one awful blow after another: the Philippines,

Guam, Wake Island, Midway Island. "The casualty lists of these first few days will undoubtedly be large." The president ended this Fireside Chat with an unadorned promise: "We are going to win the war and we are going to win the peace that follows." But for the moment, for the immediate future, he could promise nothing more than to share the news, bad and good: "This government will put its trust in the stamina of the American people, and will give the facts to the public just as soon as two conditions have been fulfilled: first, that the information has been definitely and officially confirmed; and second, that the release of the information at the time it is received will not prove valuable to the enemy directly or indirectly." There could be no greater demonstration than this that "We are all in it—all the way."

WHEN

"It will end just as soon as we make it end . . ."

—Ninth annual message to Congress, January 6, 1942

At the start of any great undertaking or in the midst of a crisis, people look for direction. That is only natural, and it is the leader's task to provide that leadership. But part of leadership is the leader's understanding that he cannot take on *all* jobs and responsibilities and that he cannot make *all* of the decisions *all* of the time. He wants a collaborative team, not a brigade of robots or slavish followers. So at key points and on issues of strategic importance, the leader must be able to turn back upon the organization some part of the authority that organization naturally invests in him.

"Many people ask," FDR remarked to Congress in his ninth annual message, " 'When will this war end?' "

Here was a huge question. To attempt an answer would have required Roosevelt to take on a responsibility no leader could have accepted one month after Pearl Harbor. On the other hand to have answered simply "I don't know" would have been truthful but it would also have been an abandonment of leadership. Instead of either taking on the burden of an answer or refusing one,

Roosevelt turned back upon the American people the question and all it implied:

> There is only one answer to that. It will end just as soon as we make it end, by our combined efforts, our combined strength, our combined determination to fight through and work through until the end—the end of militarism in Germany and Italy and Japan. Most certainly we shall not settle for less.

This was a genuine answer, but it was not an easy answer in that it refused to relieve the organization of its responsibility.

No leader can deliver a more powerful or more empowering message than to transform "I" and "you" into "we" and then declare: "*We* are the answer—the *only* answer."

MAKE EVERYONE COUNT
AND ACCOUNTABLE

"Let no man say it cannot be done. It must be done—and we have undertaken to do it."

—Ninth annual message to Congress, January 6, 1942

"This [wartime industrial] production of ours in the United States must be raised far above present levels, even though it will mean the dislocation of the lives and occupations of millions of our own people," President Roosevelt advised Congress.

> Our task is hard—our task is unprecedented—and the time is short. We must strain every existing armament-producing facility to the utmost. We must convert every available plant and tool to war production. That goes all the way from the greatest plants to the smallest—from the huge automobile industry to the village machine shop.
>
> Production for war is based on men and women—the human hands and brains which collectively we call Labor.

The war effort is not just the business of big government, of big industry, of a big military, but of every man and woman, and it depends on the faith and confidence of every individual as well: "Let no man say it cannot be done. It must be done—and we have undertaken to do it."

To mobilize action effectively, a leader creates unity while simultaneously addressing the effort, contribution, and accountability of each member of the group. Cohesiveness of purpose is essential, but a leader must never forget that it is not a company, a department, or an organization that he leads, but individual human beings gathered for a common purpose.

COUNT THEM IN

". . . even the small gardens helped."

—Statement urging the growing of victory gardens

Victory gardens were a homefront feature of both world wars. All across America, people turned garden plots, large and sometimes as small as window boxes, into gardens for growing vegetables that a family could consume instead buying vegetables at the store. In this way food was conserved, more food could be supplied for use by the troops, and the war effort reaped the benefit. Moreover by decreasing the homefront demand for certain produce, prices were more readily kept in line, and shortages caused by wartime inflation avoided.

That, at least, was the theory. And although victory gardens were immensely popular, most Americans probably thought of them as make-work, something to get everyone that much more involved in the war.

This in fact was the case; for such inclusive activities, which engage as many as possible in the collective effort, are indeed valuable. But Roosevelt took pains to point out that the victory gardens made a real, significant, and indeed, *quantifiable* impact on the war effort. The statement he issued on the subject, short and to-the-point, but filled with all of the relevant facts, is vintage

FDR because in it he made certain that when it came to the great national enterprise of World War II, *everyone* was counted in:

> I hope every American who possibly can will grow a victory garden this year. We found out last year that even the small gardens helped.
>
> The total harvest from victory gardens was tremendous. It made the difference between scarcity and abundance. The Department of Agriculture surveys show that 42 percent of the fresh vegetables consumed in 1943 came from victory gardens. This should clearly emphasize the far-reaching importance of the victory garden program.
>
> Because of the greatly increased demands in 1944, we will need all the food we can grow. Food still remains a first essential to winning the war. Victory gardens are of direct benefit in helping relieve manpower, transportation, and living costs as well as the food problem. Increased food requirements for our armed forces and our allies give every citizen an opportunity to do something toward backing up the boys at the front.

The commander in chief at sea.
(Image from the Library of Congress.)

With Free French leader Charles de Gaulle and
Britain's Prime Minister Winston Churchill at
the Casablanca Conference, January 1943.
(Image from the Library of Congress.)

The president meets with Joe McQueen of the Disabled American Veterans organization. FDR well understood disability and what it took to live with it and to overcome it.

Allies: Canadian Prime Minister William Lyon Mackenzie with FDR.

Allies: Soviet commissar of foreign affairs Vyacheslav Mikhaylovich Molotov with FDR.

Allies: Madame Chiang Kai-shek, the beautiful, powerful, popular, and persuasive wife of Nationalist China's Generalissimo Chiang Kai-shek, with FDR.

Official photograph from the 1930s. Millions of these hung in government offices, private offices, stores, and homes throughout the Depression and World War II.

FDR was a favorite subject of mostly good-natured caricature. This one is by popular Latin dance-orchestra leader Xavier Cugat.

A charcoal study by the artist Enit Kaufman.

Patriotic portrait from the war years.
(Image from the National Archives and Records Administration.)

The president attends his last wartime conference, at Yalta in the Crimea, February 1945. He is pictured here with Ibn Saud, king of Saudi Arabia.

FDR did not live to complete his fourth term. He died of a cerebral hemorrhage on April 12, 1945. After he was sworn in, Harry S. Truman confided to reporters, "Boys, if you ever pray, pray for me now. I don't know whether you fellows ever had a load of hay fall on you, but when they told me yesterday what had happened, I felt like the moon, the stars, and all the planets had fallen on me."

The funeral cortege of Franklin Delano Roosevelt.
(Images from the Library of Congress.)

ON SELF-INTEREST AND SELF-SACRIFICE

CREATE A POSITIVE SPIN

"I always like to emphasize the word privilege *rather than the word* duty.*"*

—Address to the Conference on the Mobilization for
Human Needs, September 28, 1934

On September 28, 1934, the Conference on the Mobilization for Human Needs convened for a second time, at the invitation of the president, in the White House. FDR reminded the members of the organization that "last year" he had observed that "the primary responsibility for community needs rests upon the community itself." He went on to praise the Mobilization for Human Needs for taking up this responsibility, which he carefully defined not as a "duty," but a "privilege":

> for it is clearly the privilege of the individual American to bear his personal share in a work which must be kept personal insofar as it is possible to make it so. It is that personal appeal, that personal service, which has carried us through all these trying years.

Almost always near the top of a leader's list of tasks is to secure compliance from those he leads—the more enthusiastic, creative, and spirited that compliance, the better. It is therefore in the best interest of the enterprise for the leader to spin the concept of compliance—duty—as positively as possible, even revealing it as a privilege rather than a requirement or burden.

As Roosevelt put it here, this interpretation is no mere donning of rose-colored glasses, but a thoughtful and thought-provoking observation. Why should it "clearly" be a "privilege of the individual American to bear his personal share" in the work of national economic recovery? FDR did not connect all the dots for us but instead required us to do the thinking for ourselves. The greatness of the American enterprise is individual liberty, and the ultimate evidence of that liberty is the individual responsibility that goes with it. America gives one the space to act personally and directly, to affect the lives of others, to make a difference. As a leader during crisis, Roosevelt understood the necessity of introducing central government into individual lives to an unprecedented degree. But in doing so he wanted above all else to avoid damaging the spirit of individual liberty and responsibility that is essential to a democracy. Thus as a leader, even in crisis, FDR sought to underscore and affirm that American individuality, even as he asked for a new degree of unified action and cooperation. The bridge between individualism and collective action is the concept of privilege: the privilege—not the coerced duty—of the individual to shoulder the burden of helping other individuals. The *effective* leader always seeks the most positive possible definition of the individual's role in the collective enterprise. The *great* leader does this in a way that strikes those he leads as self-evident, that elicits not a cynical shake of the head but enthusiastic assent.

DO WELL BY DOING GOOD

"We have always known that heedless self-interest was bad for morals; we know now that it is bad economics."

—Second inaugural address, January 20, 1937

"Old truths," President Roosevelt declared at his second inauguration, explaining the lessons of his first term, "have been relearned; untruths have been unlearned." For example: "We have always known that heedless self-interest was bad for morals; we know now that it is bad economics."

Too many of us fail to see that all business is, in essence, exchange. There are no one-way transactions in business. A one-way transaction is not business, but theft. Everything is reciprocal. Take the longer view, and the world of business emerges as a system of reciprocal transactions. In business, as in life itself, "self-interest" is natural and healthy. It contributes to survival. However, "heedless self-interest" focuses exclusively on the self, forgetting that personal survival and prosperity depend on the survival and prosperity of others. This is bad morality because it creates pain and poverty for one's neighbors and it is bad economics because it dooms oneself to failure. It is difficult to do business in a market without means.

Heedless self-interest is a fatally limited view. Take in the whole picture, and you will act from motives beyond immediate self-interest, not just because doing so satisfies your moral instincts, but because it is manifestly and obviously good business. An effective leader always leads us to this whole-picture view.

TOO MUCH POWER

"In the face of the danger which confronts our time, no individual retains, or can hope to retain, the right of personal choice which free men enjoy in times of peace."

—Radio address to the 1940 Democratic National Convention, July 19, 1940

Serving in precedent-shattering times, Franklin Roosevelt destroyed many of those precedents, even as he couched his actions and initiatives in the historical and traditional context of supporting American ideals. None of the shattered precedents was more dramatic or more controversial than his successful run for a third term in office. Ever since George Washington declined a third term, the two-term limit had been quite literally an unwritten law, which no chief executive had ever before made bold to break (unless we count Theodore Roosevelt's 1912 "Bull Moose" run as a genuine third-party candidacy). But FDR believed that he was the right leader for a nation emerging from one protracted crisis—the Great Depression—and verging on another, World War II. His party agreed, and he stood for a third term.

Americans wanted FDR to remain in the White House, and he defeated Republican Wendell Wilkie by capturing 54.7 percent of the vote to Wilkie's 44.8 percent. Yet public opinion was widespread that two terms were enough for any president and that to serve for longer than eight years invited the creation of a dictatorship. Was Roosevelt power hungry?

FDR believed it was necessary to address those who questioned the wisdom of a third term, yet he understood that in addressing this issue, there was a real danger of appearing overly defensive. In Shakespeare's *Macbeth,* Lady Macbeth's guilty feelings are made manifest by her repeated protestations of innocence: "The lady doth protest too much," we are told. And so FDR put the third-term issue in a new light:

> It is with a very full heart that I speak tonight. I must confess that I do so with mixed feelings—because I find myself, as almost everyone does sooner or later in his lifetime, in a conflict between deep personal desire for retirement on the one hand, and that quiet, invisible thing called "conscience" on the other.
>
> . . . Eight years in the presidency, following a period of bleak depression, and covering one world crisis after another, would normally entitle any man to the relaxation that comes from honorable retirement.

In this instance he portrayed himself to the public not as a leader but as a man, one who has, in strictly personal terms, earned his rest. In this way he shifted the issue of a third term from one of continuing to take and hold power to one of conscience, service, duty, and self-sacrifice:

> In the face of the danger which confronts our time, no individual retains, or can hope to retain, the right of personal choice which free men enjoy in times of peace. He has a first obligation to serve in the defense of our institutions of freedom—a first obligation to

serve his country in whatever capacity his country finds him useful.

Like most men of my age, I had plans for myself, plans for a private life of my own choice and for my own satisfaction, a life of that kind to begin in January 1941. These plans, like so many other plans, had been made in a world which now seems as distant as another planet. Today all private plans, all private lives, have been in a sense repealed by an overriding public danger. In the face of that public danger all those who can be of service to the Republic have no choice but to offer themselves for service in those capacities for which they may be fitted.

Not only was FDR able to redefine the issue of the third term with these remarks, he also set himself up as an example of the kind of self-sacrifice, service, and commitment to duty he knew would be required of all Americans in the coming years.

As persuasive as FDR's argument justifying a third term was— and he went on to a fourth, as well—the American people remained properly wary of investing so much power for so long in one person. FDR was manifestly a good man, genuinely dedicated to service. But what guarantee was there that the next person to seek a third term would be so selfless? In 1951 ratification of the Twenty-second Amendment to the Constitution barred election "to the office of the President more than twice."

TAKE THE SELFISH POINT OF VIEW

"I am talking selfishly, from the American point of view—nothing else."

—Press conference on lend-lease, December 17, 1940

In 1940, the United States was still officially neutral in World War II, but Franklin Roosevelt (and others) recognized that it was in the best interest of the nation to aid Great Britain against the Axis forces. President Roosevelt championed a lend-lease policy, whereby Britain (and then China, the USSR, and other nations as well) would be supplied with urgently needed war matériel, not on a cash-and-carry basis, but in exchange for payment "in kind or property, or any other direct or indirect benefit," as the president saw fit. In a celebrated figure of speech, FDR explained the principle of lend-lease this way:

> Suppose my neighbor's home catches fire, and I have got a length of garden hose four or five hundred feet away; but, by Heaven, if he can take my garden hose and connect it up with his hydrant, I may help him to put out his fire. Now, what do I do? I don't say to him before that operation, "Neighbor, my garden hose cost

me $15; you have got to pay me $15 for it." What is the transaction that goes on? I don't want $15—I want my garden hose back after the fire is over. All right. If it goes through the fire all right, intact, without any damage to it, he gives it back to me and thanks me very much for the use of it. But suppose it gets smashed up—holes in it—during the fire; we don't have to have too much formality about it, but I say to him, "I was glad to lend you that hose; I see I can't use it any more, it's all smashed up." He says, "How many feet of it were there?" I tell him, "There were 150 feet of it." He says, "All right, I will replace it." Now, if I get a nice garden hose back, I am in pretty good shape. In other words, if you lend certain munitions and get the munitions back at the end of the war, if they are intact—haven't been hurt—you are all right; if they have been damaged or deteriorated or lost completely, it seems to me you come out pretty well if you have them replaced by the fellow that you have lent them to.

Roosevelt could have elaborated on the homely analogy a bit further, posing the question "What happens if you don't lend your neighbor the hose, and his house goes up in flames?" The answer is that the fire might well spread out of control to your house as well. FDR didn't draw the analogy this far, to illustrate the selfish motive in helping your neighbor but he did focus on that selfish motive. Lend-lease *sounds* like giving something away, making a sacrifice in return for nothing. FDR did not address this issue by appealing to American altruism, a feeling that we should stand up for good old Britain in its struggle against Hitler. Instead he pointed out that "the best immediate defense of the United States is the success of Great Britain in defending itself," so that, "quite aside from our historic and current interest in the survival of democracy as a whole in the world, it is equally important from a selfish point of view of American defense that we should do everything to help the British Empire to defend itself."

Not only is Britain a bulwark against a grave menace to our own shores, but the war-matériel orders from Great Britain are "a tremendous asset to American national defense, because they create, automatically, additional facilities. I am talking selfishly, from the American point of view—nothing else. Therefore, from the selfish point of view, that production must be encouraged by us . . ."

The leadership point is this: Appeal to your organization's spirit of self-sacrifice and you may well be gratifyingly *surprised* by a positive response. But appeal to its self-interest—to its selfishness—and you will never be surprised. You can be *assured* of a positive response.

SELL BENEFIT, NOT COST

"It is not a sacrifice for any man, old or young, to be in the army or navy of the United States. Rather is it a privilege."

—Fireside Chat on war with Japan, December 9, 1941

Among a leader's responsibilities is leading her enterprise to the truth of any particular situation. Yet the fact is that in most situations of even an elementary degree of complexity, there is not one truth but several, perhaps even many. Indeed, "truth," in most human situations, is not a single thing, but a matter of perspective. Thus a leader's job is often to influence the perspective from which the members of her enterprise view the situation at hand.

President Roosevelt found himself the leader of a nation at war. In his Fireside Chat of December 9, 1941, two days after Pearl Harbor, he leveled with the American people, as he always did: "On the road ahead there lies hard work—grueling work—day and night, every hour and every minute." It is a sentence worthy of that other great wartime leader, Winston Churchill, who stirred the Parliament and the people of England with this grim promise: "I have nothing to offer but blood, toil, tears and sweat."

Like Churchill, Roosevelt placed his faith in the strength, the courage, and the stamina of a free people. Like Churchill, Roosevelt used the concept of self-sacrifice to stir the nation. But in contrast to Churchill, Roosevelt added a stroke of American sales-manship, which invited his listeners to look at the truth of sacri-fice from a new perspective:

> I was about to add that ahead there lies sacrifice for all of us.
>
> But it is not correct to use that word. The United States does not consider it a sacrifice to do all one can, to give one's best to our nation, when the nation is fighting for its existence and its future life.
>
> It is not a sacrifice for any man, old or young, to be in the army or navy of the United States. Rather is it a privilege.
>
> It is not a sacrifice for the industrialist or the wage earner, the farmer or the shopkeeper, the trainman or the doctor, to pay more taxes, to buy more bonds, to forego extra profits, to work longer or harder at the task for which he is best fitted. Rather is it a privilege.
>
> It is not a sacrifice to do without many things to which we are accustomed if the national defense calls for doing without.

Anyone who makes a living selling quickly learns that it is poor salesmanship to dwell on the cost of the product. Instead you fo-cus on its value and benefit. This is neither a distortion nor a lie, but merely a matter of perspective. Cost, value, and benefit are all truths or aspects of the truth about a given product. The effective salesperson leads the customer to the perspective of value and benefit and away from the perspective of cost.

Similarly, Roosevelt, while hiding nothing about the hard road ahead, adjusted the perspective on that truth by focusing not on sacrifice as loss, but on sacrifice as privilege. He directed America's attention to the value and benefit of sacrifice, rather than to its cost.

THEME TWELVE

ON CONFIDENCE AND COURAGE

THE ONLY THING WE HAVE TO FEAR

"This great nation will endure as it has endured, will revive and will prosper. So, first of all, let me assert my firm belief that the only thing we have to fear is fear itself—nameless, unreasoning, unjustified terror which paralyzes needed efforts to convert retreat into advance."

—First inaugural address, March 4, 1933

In *Defending Your Life,* a charmingly provocative 1991 movie written and directed by its star, Albert Brooks, we discover that the only truly unforgivable sin in life is fear. Killed in a head-on crash with a bus, yuppie Brooks finds himself transported to Judgment City, where he must "defend his life" before a pair of judges who will decide whether he is to be returned to Earth for another crack at life or be permitted to progress to the next plane of existence. His attorney (for the benevolent managers of the universe provide defense assistance) explains to him the nature of fear, which is, he says, a "fog" that obscures everything and that makes intelligent, productive action impossible.

It is a stimulating thought—that fear is not so much the sensation accompanying the realization of danger, but a fog, an obscurer of truth, an interference with how we may productively

213

engage reality. Certainly this is the way FDR saw it. In 1921 polio threatened first to kill him and then paralyzed him, subjected him to a life of relentless pain, and nearly ended his career in public service. He could then and there have given in to the fog of fear, but he chose not to. He chose instead to understand polio, to see clearly the extent of his disability, and then to assess—also clearly—his options for overcoming that disability. He did not blink at the odds. He looked at them, contemplated them, assessed them, and then acted on them.

Now, more than a decade later, assuming the office of president of the United States, he began by asking the American people to sweep aside the fog of fear, "nameless, unreasoning, unjustified terror which paralyzes needed efforts to convert retreat into advance." He didn't ask them to stop being afraid, but to stop letting fear obscure their vision of reality. He asked the people to confront what they feared, so that they could see clearly what needed to be done and thereby overcome (and the word is significant) the terror that *paralyzes*.

In the second paragraph of his inaugural speech, FDR lifted the fog of fear. What did he reveal to his audience, the American people?

> Values have shrunken to fantastic levels; taxes have risen; our ability to pay has fallen; government of all kinds is faced by serious curtailment of income; the means of exchange are frozen in the currents of trade; the withered leaves of industrial enterprise lie on every side; farmers find no markets for their produce; the savings of many years in thousands of families are gone.

There is no sugarcoating of reality here! The fog has lifted, the scene is sharply etched and downright frightening: "a host of unemployed citizens face the grim problem of existence, and an

equally great number toil with little return. Only a foolish optimist can deny the dark realities of the moment."

FDR did not blink at reality and he did not allow his audience
to do so either. He embarked on this catalog of economic disasters
by defining them as "our common difficulties," which "concern,
thank God, only material things."

The fog was lifted and the president's listeners could see the reality they already knew, a reality of poverty and despair, to be sure;
yet with the fog of fear lifted, they could see it in a new light: Our
common difficulties "concern, thank God, only material things."

Not one to blink at disaster, FDR also saw a way out of it:

> Yet our distress comes from no failure of substance. We
> are stricken by no plague of locusts. Compared with
> the perils which our forefathers conquered because they
> believed and were not afraid, we have still much to be
> thankful for. Nature still offers her bounty and human
> efforts have multiplied it. Plenty is at our doorstep . . .

Lift the fog of fear and you could see that the Great Depression
was not of natural, supernatural, or inevitable origin. It was not a
plague of biblical proportion. Our kind has conquered worse in
the past. Nature has not failed us.

What, then, was the problem?

> Plenty is at our doorstep, but a generous use of it lan-
> guishes in the very sight of the supply. Primarily this is
> because rulers of the exchange of mankind's good have
> failed through their own stubbornness and their own
> incompetence, have admitted their failure, and have
> abdicated. Practices of unscrupulous money changers
> stand indicted in the court of public opinion, rejected
> by the hearts and minds of men.

The failure was a failure of particular human beings and the particular policies they pursued. "True," Roosevelt continued, these particular people "have tried, but their efforts have been cast in the pattern of an outworn tradition."

> Faced by failure of credit they have proposed only the lending of more money. Stripped of the lure of profit by which to induce our people to follow their false leadership, they have resorted to exhortation, pleading tearfully for restored confidence. They know only the rules of a generation of self-seekers. They have no vision, and when there is no vision the people perish.

As a leader FDR always navigated between the radically new and unprecedented, on the one hand, and the age-old and unchanging, on the other. Early in the speech he evoked the Old Testament image of a plague of locusts. He used another biblical image, this one from the New Testament, in referring to the "unscrupulous money changers." Then he went on to speak of the Depression as a problem created by old ways of thinking. It was, he said, a problem that could not be solved by "efforts . . . cast in the pattern of outworn tradition," the pattern of a "generation of self-seekers."

The implication was unmistakable: Conquering the Depression would require new thinking. And yet FDR once again linked this need for fresh imagination and bold, new action with the timeless wisdom of Judeo-Christian tradition. In Proverbs 29:18 we are told, "Where there is no vision, the people perish," and FDR tells us that the Depression was created and is perpetuated by leaders who "have no vision, and when there is no vision the people perish." He continued with his echo of the Gospels:

> The money changers have fled from their high seats in the temple of our civilization. We may now restore that

temple to the ancient truths. The measure of the restoration lies in the extent to which we apply social values more noble than mere monetary profit.

An inauguration is a beginning, as Roosevelt was well aware, and in his acceptance speech to the Democratic National Convention, he had already pledged to the American people a "New Deal." Americans would soon discover, during the dazzling first hundred days of the Roosevelt presidency, just how new a deal it would be, as program after innovative program was ushered into being. Yet all of this innovation was aimed at restoring the "temple of our civilization . . . to the ancient truths," the age-old redemption of the temple of the spirit from the grasp of the materialistic money changers.

> Happiness lies not in the mere possession of money; it lies in the joy of achievement, in the thrill of creative effort. The joy and moral stimulation of work no longer must be forgotten in the mad chase of evanescent profits. These dark days will be worth all they cost us if they teach us that our true destiny is not to be ministered unto but to minister to ourselves and our fellow men.

Here then, in the space of the first few minutes of his first speech as leader of the American people, is what Franklin Roosevelt made visible in the absence of the fog of fear: that the economic disaster is serious, urgent, even life-threatening, *yet* it is an *economic* disaster, one concerning "thank God, only material things." Roosevelt's speech does not allow his listeners to turn away from the disaster. His words invite them to see beyond it, both to its cause in human errors, in the shortsighted pursuit of immediate material profit, and in the absence of greater vision, to its eventual resolution.

That resolution is the subject of the rest of the speech, which broadly outlines innovative goals, policies, and programs aimed at ending the Great Depression. Yet the proposed means of resolution, radical as they may be, rest on restoring the "temple of our civilization . . . to the ancient truths." Paramount among these truths is a realization that "happiness lies not in the mere possession of money," that morals and ethics must not be sacrificed in "the mad chase of evanescent profits," and that our "true destiny is not to be ministered unto but to minister to ourselves and our fellow men."

KEEP THE FAITH

"There are men who doubt . . ."

—Third inaugural address, January 20, 1941

"Lives of nations are determined not by the count of years," Franklin Roosevelt declared at his third inauguration, "but by the lifetime of the human spirit."

> The life of a man is threescore years and ten: a little more, a little less. The life of a nation is the fullness of the measure of its will to live.
>
> There are men who doubt this. There are men who believe that democracy, as a form of government and a frame of life, is limited or measured by a kind of mystical and artificial fate—that, for some unexplained reason, tyranny and slavery have become the surging wave of the future—and that freedom is an ebbing tide.

FDR almost never stated just one side of an issue, nor did he customarily view reality from a single perspective. In his third inaugural address he presented his lofty view of the link between a nation's spirit and the human spirit, then, with equal eloquence, presented the contrary view, a view apparently supported all too compellingly by the dismal events in the world of 1939–41. After all, what sane and sentient being would *not* have doubts, on January 20, 1941, concerning the fate of democracy? Hitler's Germany was goose-stepping across Europe, and militaristic Japan was ravaging Asia.

Yet FDR found even more compelling facts to counter the view of the "men who doubt." To those who believed "that freedom is an ebbing tide," Roosevelt replied:

> But we Americans know that this is not true.
>
> Eight years ago, when the life of this Republic seemed frozen by a fatalistic terror, we proved that this is not true. We were in the midst of shock—but we acted. We acted quickly, boldly, decisively.
>
> These later years have been living years—fruitful years for the people of this democracy.

The refutation of the doubters' facts was to be found in the more compelling facts of the nation's victory over the Great Depression, which, like the apparent triumph of the dictators, had been seen as the herald of the failure of democracy. A great leader may build for the future but he does so by building in the present and upon the past. He maintains the vital links that connect experience with present action and future expectation.

TO THE TIMID ONES

"Never in the history of the world has a nation lost its democracy by a successful struggle to defend its democracy."

—Radio address announcing an unlimited
national emergency, May 27, 1941

Almost all groups, from the humblest corporate teams to great nations, are innately conservative, preferring, if at all possible, to avoid risk, bold action, or a fight. This is not the result of collective cowardice but of a conviction that the safest, soundest course is always the most conservative—that is, the least active.

FDR understood that a passion for inaction gives only the illusion of security.

> There are some timid ones among us who say that we must preserve peace at any price—lest we lose our liberties forever. To them I say this: Never in the history of the world has a nation lost its democracy by a successful struggle to defend its democracy. . . . Our freedom has shown its ability to survive war, but our freedom would never survive surrender.

In any enterprise threat must be recognized. Once acknowledged it must also be understood that inaction in the face of threat is surrender, not safety. An effective leader always makes the stakes clear. Choosing to fight is dangerous, to be sure, but in many situations opting for the apparently safer course of hunkering down in resolute inaction is simply defeat—the very consequence one fears in a fight.

Illusion aside, it is a fate far more terrible and terrifying to await defeat quietly than to engage the enemy—the rival, the problem—in a determined, well-planned, and well-executed struggle.

TURN TACTICAL DEFEAT
INTO STRATEGIC TRIUMPH

*". . . always will our whole nation remember the character of
the onslaught against us."*

—Address before Congress requesting a declaration of
war against Japan, December 8, 1941

No Roosevelt speech is more famous than that of December 8,
1941. Perhaps no American speech, save the Gettysburg Address,
is more familiar. And until the September 11, 2001, terrorist attacks on the World Trade Center and the Pentagon, no assault
against the United States was more shocking or terrible than the
Japanese surprise attack of December 7, 1941, on Pearl Harbor,
Hawaii.

Having lived through the attacks of September 11, 2001,
those of our generation need no longer merely imagine what
Americans felt in 1941 when they learned that on Sunday at 7:50
in the morning, carrier-launched Japanese aircraft staged an in-
tensive two-hour attack that left eighteen U.S. ships sunk or badly
damaged and more than two hundred aircraft destroyed on the
ground. The great battleships *Arizona, West Virginia, Oklahoma,*
and *California* were destroyed, and the *Nevada* was severely mauled.
Some 2,400 U.S. military personnel were killed, 1,300 wounded,
and 1,000 missing. The single bright spot in this military disaster

was that the American aircraft carrier fleet was at sea, not in port, and therefore escaped damage. Subsequent U.S. naval operations would hinge on those carriers.

There can be no denying that the Pearl Harbor attack was superbly executed. For the Japanese it was a tactical triumph—and yet also a terrible strategic defeat. As the historian Samuel Eliot Morison later wrote, "one can search military history in vain for an operation more fatal to the aggressor."

Tactics are about immediate objectives and results. Strategy takes the long view. It is, as the well-worn cliché has it, quite possible to win a battle yet lose the war. Of course, it is easy for a historian, gifted with hindsight, to appreciate how an immediate tactical victory can spell ultimate strategic defeat. Morison knew that December 7, 1941, galvanized American resolve, instantly focusing the will and resources of a great nation in a boundless effort to defeat the aggressor and its allies. Such an insight was immeasurably more difficult for the leader who actually lived through December 7 and who addressed Congress and the nation on the eighth. But FDR recognized that this tactical disaster for the United States carried the seeds of final victory, and it is precisely this insight that drove Roosevelt's first speech of America's second world war.

A great leader makes use of everything that happens, good, bad, triumphant, disastrous. FDR began with the event itself, describing it with that ringing word "infamy":

> Yesterday, December 7, 1941—a date which will live in infamy—the United States of America was suddenly and deliberately attacked by naval and air forces of the Empire of Japan.

FDR gave careful thought to the word. The draft typescript of the speech, which is preserved in the Library of Congress, reads "a date which will live in history," but "history" is crossed out and in Roosevelt's hand, "infamy" substituted. The word means an evil or criminal act that is publicly known. Thus from the outset, Roosevelt denied the aggressor his triumph by labeling the deed as an evil public crime, not a legitimate military action. The implications were that a great injustice had been done and had to be redressed, and that the aggressor was now deserving of punishment, not merely a military response.

It is also important to take note of what FDR did *not* say in the opening paragraph of his speech. He did not specify that the attack was against a military base located in Hawaii, at the time a U.S. territory, but declared simply that it was against "the United States of America," period.

Roosevelt continued by elaborating on the infamous nature of the attack, which came without warning when the "United States was at peace with" Japan, and while the two countries were actually engaged "in conversation . . . looking toward the maintenance of peace in the Pacific." He detailed how it "will be recorded that the distance of Hawaii from Japan makes it obvious that the attack was deliberately planned many days or even weeks ago," and that during "the intervening time the Japanese government deliberately sought to deceive the United States by false statements and expressions of continued peace."

Now, having established the treacherous, criminal, *infamous* nature of the attack, an immoral act, Roosevelt frankly faced the extent of the destruction it caused: "severe damage to American naval and military forces. I regret to tell you that very many American lives have been lost." And it only got worse:

> In addition American ships have been reported torpedoed on the high seas between San Francisco and Honolulu.
>
> Yesterday the Japanese government also launched an attack against Malaya.
>
> Last night Japanese forces attacked Hong Kong.
>
> Last night Japanese forces attacked Guam.

Last night Japanese forces attacked the Philippine Islands.

Last night Japanese forces attacked Wake Island.

And this morning the Japanese attacked Midway Island.

For Roosevelt, this catalog of defeat and disaster served two immediate purposes. First, it indicated and proved the extent of the threat, nothing less than a "surprise offensive extending throughout the Pacific area." Having presented the evidence, FDR allowed the people to evaluate it for themselves: "The people of the United States have already formed their opinions and well understand the implications to the very life and safety of our nation." He did not tell his listeners what to think. *See for yourself* is always a powerful leadership technique.

The second purpose of reporting one disaster after another was to signal to the American people that this leader would pull no punches and would hide nothing. In a time of crisis Roosevelt did what he had always done in other times of crisis: He leveled with those he led.

But it would have been a leadership catastrophe to let the catalog of defeat stand as the centerpiece of the speech. After a single sentence devoted to what he "as commander in chief of the army and navy" has done—"I have directed that all measures be taken for our defense"—Roosevelt turned the focus from *his* power and authority to that of the *people:*

But always will our whole nation remember the character of the onslaught against us.

No matter how long it may take us to overcome this premeditated invasion, the American people in their righteous might will win through to absolute victory.

The attack on Pearl Harbor—in the moment a terrible disaster—is transformed into a powerful catalyst for the "righteous might" of the American people, a formula for "absolute victory."

Roosevelt was not content to confine his message to a call to the defense of the nation: "I believe that I interpret the will of the Congress and of the people when I assert that we will not only defend ourselves to the uttermost but will make it very certain that this form of treachery shall never again endanger us." By looking beyond the attack and the immediate need for defense, Roosevelt assured the American people that they did indeed *have* a future and that a successful response to the attack on Pearl Harbor was not merely reactive, but proactive and positive. Yes, the situation was urgent and dangerous—"Hostilities exist. There is no blinking at the fact that our people, our territory, and our interests are in grave danger"—but the future promised "inevitable triumph":

> With confidence in our armed forces, with the unbounding determination of our people, we will gain the inevitable triumph—so help us God.

In the space of a three- or four-minute speech, Roosevelt led us from evident and abject defeat, an attack so one-sided it hardly deserved to be called a battle, to "inevitable triumph"—and not just inevitable triumph, but a final victory actually engendered by the present infamous disaster.

Nothing is hidden or softened. The defeat is terrible, and we are shown that. But we are led beyond it, and as real as defeat now is, we are shown the certainty of victory, inevitable and ultimate. To see beyond the smoke, the debris, the devastation—this is leadership.

ON KNOWLEDGE AND SELF-KNOWLEDGE

LESSON LEARNED

"If we learned anything from the depression we will not allow ourselves to run around in new circles of futile discussion and debate, always postponing the day of decision."

—Fireside Chat on reorganization of the judiciary, March 9, 1937

Roosevelt embarked on his second term as president determined not to allow the pace of his New Deal reforms to flag. He saw as a major obstacle, however, the Supreme Court, whose aged and conservative majority were inclined to allow New Deal legislation very little latitude where questions of constitutionality were concerned. FDR hit on a bold, innovative, highly controversial, and indeed ultimately unsuccessful solution. On February 5, 1937, he introduced the Judiciary Reorganization Bill. Opponents—and there were many—called it, with considerable justification, something else: a court-packing scheme.

The bill proposed to add judges at all levels of the federal courts, assign judges to the more congested courts, and adopt procedures to expedite the appeals process by sending lower court cases on constitutional matters directly to the Supreme Court. This was not unreasonable, many agreed, but the bill also proposed to allow justices of the Supreme Court who reached age seventy to retire with full pay. If a justice chose not to retire at seventy, the president would be authorized to appoint an additional judge—up to six in all, potentially increasing the Supreme Court to fifteen members. Although Congress quickly passed a Supreme Court Retirement Act, permitting Supreme Court Justices to retire at age seventy with full pay (after ten years of service), the court-packing scheme failed. The president was permitted to appoint a new justice *only* if the current justice actually retired. Even most partisans of FDR today agree that this failure was probably a very good thing for Constitution and country.

Typically, FDR explained controversial matters to the American people in a Fireside Chat. He used this forum to promote his Judiciary Reorganization Bill and he presented the measure as the result of lessons learned from mistakes of the past:

> Today we are only part-way through that program [of national recovery legislation]—and recovery is speeding up to a point where the dangers of 1929 are again becoming possible, not this week or month perhaps, but within a year or two. . . . If we learned anything from the depression we will not allow ourselves to run around in new circles of futile discussion and debate, always postponing the day of decision.
>
> The American people have learned from the depression. For in the last three national elections an overwhelming majority of them voted a mandate that the Congress and the president begin the task of providing that protection [against the kind of policies and practices that caused the economic collapse of 1929]— not after long years of debate, but now.
>
> The courts, however, have cast doubts on the ability of the elected Congress to protect us against catastrophe by meeting squarely our modern social and economic conditions.

Leadership requires a double focus, on the present and on the future. Often it also requires a third lens, focused on the past. If an effective leader serves as the monitor and mirror of the present situation and as a firm guide to future direction, she must also sometimes serve as the collective memory of the group, organization, or enterprise she leads. The well-worn cliché that history repeats itself is fairly meaningless folklore, but the more thoughtful observation of the philosopher George Santayana that "Those who cannot remember the past are condemned to repeat it" rings true. This does not, however, relieve the leader of the responsibility to use the lessons of the past wisely, as guides rather than dictators of present policy and future plans.

NEW THREATS AS OLD EVILS

"They are not new, my friends, they are only a relapse—a relapse into ancient history."

> —Radio address to the 1940 Democratic
> National Convention, July 19, 1940

President Roosevelt often had to champion new, even radical, programs and ideas. Generally he did so by emphasizing not their untested novelty, but their connection to traditional American policy and timeless guidelines of ethics and morality. His usual message was this: The modalities and methods might be new, designed to deal with new realities but they proceed nevertheless from time-tested principles.

In confronting an age of "great dictators"—especially of Hitler and Mussolini in Germany and Italy—FDR took head-on the excuse many had offered for tyranny: "In Europe, many nations, through dictatorships or invasions, have been compelled to abandon normal democratic processes. They have been compelled to adopt forms of government which some call 'new and efficient.'" Roosevelt countered:

> They are not new, my friends, they are only a relapse—
> a relapse into ancient history. The omnipotent rulers of

234

the greater part of modern Europe have guaranteed efficiency, and work, and a type of security.

But the slaves who built the pyramids for the glory of the dictator pharaohs of Egypt had that kind of security, that kind of efficiency, that kind of corporative state.

So did the inhabitants of that world which extended from Britain to Persia under the undisputed rule of the proconsuls sent out from Rome.

So did the henchmen, the tradesmen, the mercenaries, and the slaves of the feudal system which dominated Europe a thousand years ago.

So did the people of those nations of Europe who received their kings and their government at the whim of the conquering Napoleon.

Whatever its new trappings and new slogans, tyranny is the oldest and most discredited rule known to history.

Roosevelt did not *tell* the American people that dictatorships were evil or that they were bound to fall. He merely denied that they were new and then he demonstrated, by a chronological recitation of historical fact, that they have visited misery, oppression, and ruin on all those who, willingly or unwillingly, have embraced them; and that far from being invincible, they have all been doomed to fail. In this way Roosevelt simultaneously presented the great menace posed by Europe's current crop of tyrants, even as he revealed their ultimate vulnerability.

A leader must often be a teacher, and no lesson is more effective than experience or that collective form of experience known as history.

STEER CLEAR OF
COLLECTIVE SELF-BLAME

"We need not harp on failure . . ."

—Eighth annual message to Congress, January 6, 1941

Historians, from the most sophisticated university professors to high school teachers, are quick to point out the connection between the harshly punitive Treaty of Versailles, which ended World War I and crushed Germany economically and spiritually, and the rise of Adolf Hitler, who promised Germans a return to might and greatness. This is not a fresh insight. Back in 1939–40, as Europe first lunged toward World War II and then commenced actual combat, politicians, commentators, and historians spoke of how the Treaty of Versailles had doomed the world to the likes of Hitler and Mussolini. In effect there was a rush to blame the victims, the targets of tyranny, for the actions of the tyrants.

Certainly there was some validity to this view, but FDR saw it as counterproductive and destructive. The defense of democracy was not well served by assuming the stance of willing or even guilty victim:

> We need not overemphasize imperfections in the Peace of Versailles. We need not harp on failure of the democracies to deal with problems of world reconstruction.

We should remember that the Peace of 1919 was far less unjust than the kind of "pacification" which began before Munich [when Britain's Neville Chamberlain attempted to appease Hitler by cutting him a slice of Czechoslovakia], and which is being carried on under the new order of tyranny that seeks to spread over every continent today.

A leader should not attempt to blind himself or those he leads to errors and flaws in the enterprise. Critical self-examination is essential to progress. Yet it is far more destructive to magnify self-criticism. You and your enterprise do not have to be perfect to be better than the problems or problem people you face. While encouraging healthy self-reflection, an effective leader also maintains the group's perspective on the positive aspects of its objectives, its performance, and its achievements.

THE TASK

"In this day the task of the people is . . ."

—Third inaugural address, January 20, 1941

Anyone chosen to lead a great enterprise is naturally the focus of attention. As the focus of attention, the leader's natural inclination is to concentrate on herself, to think about what she must do, and to explain to others what she will do.

This is normal. It is also a fundamental leadership error. For a leader's focus should be primarily outward, on the people of the enterprise and on the tasks the enterprise must take up and complete successfully. Thus in his third inaugural address, Franklin Roosevelt did not begin by speaking about himself or even about his administration but turned the focus instead on the people. His keynote was a definition of the task facing the people of the United States and, as was his custom, he couched this great and intimidating task in the context of a history of equally great and intimidating tasks already successfully completed:

> In Washington's day the task of the people was to create and weld together a nation.
>
> In Lincoln's day the task of the people was to preserve that nation from disruption from within.

238

In this day the task of the people is to save that nation and its institutions from disruption from without.

The president pulled no punches. To save a nation is no small
task. But he expressed the task as the *third* in a series of monu-
mental tasks at which the people had not failed. Moreover he presented this third task as merely a variation on the other two: create
and weld, save from internal threat, save from external threat. The
logic of the progression created a momentum of confidence sug-
gesting that, like the two previous tasks, this one would also be
completed, by us, the people, successfully. It was our heritage of
responsibility.

FDR was highly skilled at gently lowering enormous burdens
on those he led, while simultaneously inspiring in them the
strength to bear those burdens.

WHAT WE ALL HAVE LEARNED

"In these past few years—and, most violently, in the past three days—we have learned a terrible lesson."

—Fireside Chat on war with Japan, December 9, 1941

Few well-intended words are more lame, after some disaster, than "It could have been worse." But the fact is this: No matter how serious the crisis or grave the challenge, it *could* be worse. We could take nothing away from the experience; we could fail to learn from it; we could allow the blow to remain a meaningless injury.

Did the soldiers and sailors who fell at Pearl Harbor die in vain?

They might have—if, Roosevelt tells his fellow Americans, *if* we fail to heed the lesson of Pearl Harbor or "forget what we have learned."

> It is our obligation to our dead—it is our sacred obligation to their children and to our children—that we must never forget what we have learned.
>
> And what we all have learned is this:
>
> There is no such thing as security for any nation—or any individual—in a world ruled by the principles of gangsterism.

There is no such thing as impregnable defense against powerful aggressors who sneak up in the dark and strike without warning.

We have learned that our ocean-girt hemisphere is not immune from severe attack—that we cannot measure our safety in terms of miles on any map anymore.

One great measure of a leader's ability is how he manages crisis. Panic, hysterical actions, pronouncements of gloom, and the liberal issuance of accusation and blame are obviously not the elements of effective leadership.

But it is also not sufficient merely to face crisis with calm. The real test of leadership is how much value and knowledge the organization derives from disaster—the good that is mined from the bad. Approached with intelligent resolve, a crisis can furnish leverage to achievement, whereas a failure to learn from catastrophe multiplies even the worst disaster far beyond the immediate crisis.

ON PROGRESS AND PREDICTION

PRODUCE THE EVIDENCE

"Today we have reason to believe that things are a little better than they were two months ago."

—Fireside Chat on new economic policies, May 7, 1933

The next time you have to make a speech, resist the temptation to raise the volume when you reach the most important point you have to make. Instead do the opposite. Lower your voice, even to a whisper, then watch your audience concentrate on your every word.

We are accustomed to shutting out loud noises but tuning in to quiet messages. Similarly we become immune to hype and even more indifferent to hype that is hyped upon hype. Turn down the volume to express a modest but meaningful fact, however, and you have our undivided attention.

So FDR, holding the second Fireside Chat of his presidency, reported on the effect of some of the economic policies and programs already implemented and the projected effect of some yet to be introduced. He trumpeted no miracles, but spoke only of having "reason to believe things are a little better than they were two months ago," that is, on the occasion of his first Fireside Chat.

It is a modest assertion—modest, but real. How real? An effective leader is an effective communicator, who shows rather than tells: "Industry has picked up, railroads are carrying more freight, farm prices are better . . ." These are real, tangible markers, which have an impact on people's lives. But Roosevelt demurred:

> . . . I am not going to indulge in issuing proclamations of overenthusiastic assurance. We cannot ballyhoo ourselves back to prosperity. I am going to be honest at all times with the people of the country. I do not want the people of this country to take the foolish course of letting this improvement come back on another speculative wave. I do not want the people to believe that because of unjustified optimism we can resume the ruinous practice of increasing our crop output and our factory output in the hope that a kind Providence will find buyers at high prices. Such a course may bring us immediate and false prosperity but it will be the kind of prosperity that will lead us into another tailspin.

FDR was eager to preempt hype, to give hope but to avoid false hope, to mark progress but to prevent such markers from becoming guides to complacency and carelessness. Improvement and progress are great motivators, provided that the paper currency of all claims is backed by the gold and silver of fact. In this way the danger of rhetorical inflation, which quickly converts hope into despair, enthusiasm into cynicism, and confidence into doubt, may be avoided.

WE HAVE SURVIVED

"We have survived all of the arduous burdens and the threatening dangers of a great economic calamity."

—Fireside Chat on the Works Relief Program, April 28, 1935

A leader is a guide. Often the principal leadership task is to direct the enterprise into the future, but in doing this, the leader must not neglect the present. A leader marks where we are going—and where we are now. He tells us not only how far we must still travel but also makes us aware of how far we have come. And so FDR provided the nation with an assessment of its progress: "Never since my inauguration in March 1933 have I felt so unmistakably the atmosphere of recovery." This was a most hopeful assessment, and he continued to define and refine it:

> But it is more than the recovery of the material basis of our individual lives. It is the recovery of confidence in our democratic processes and institutions. We have survived all of the arduous burdens and the threatening dangers of a great economic calamity. We have in the darkest moments of our national trials retained our faith in our ability to master our destiny, fear is vanishing and confidence is growing on every side . . .

247

President Roosevelt would have been the last person to declare that victory over Depression had been won or, much less, to repeat the mantra of Herbert Hoover: "Prosperity is just around the corner." But he was eager to provide hope based on progress: progress measured in time ("since my inauguration in March 1933"), in wealth ("the material basis of our individual lives"), and, most important of all, in "confidence in our democratic processes and institutions." Did anyone demand proof of this progress? If so, FDR provided it: *We have survived.*

RAISE SPECULATION TO FACT

"No, I am not speculating about all this."

—Radio address announcing an unlimited
national emergency, May 27, 1941

Even as late as the spring of 1941, with Hitler's armies overrunning Europe and all European democracies defeated save England, Roosevelt was faced with the task of waking a vast number of American isolationists to the reality of world war and the urgent necessity of preparing for it.

Prediction and speculation are often necessary in leading any enterprise. Future developments, trends, problems, opportunities, and challenges must be anticipated. And yet speculation is always inherently weak as a persuader. Present a speculation, even a probable one, and this counterargument can always be offered: *Yes, it* might *happen. But, then, it* might *not.* The best—the most persuasive—leadership strategy is to find ways of moving speculation as close as possible to fact. In his radio address, FDR did just this. He presented a picture of the Americas subject to a Hitler allowed to run rampant. "Germany would literally parcel out the world," Roosevelt warned, "hoisting the swastika itself over vast territories and populations, and setting up puppet governments of its own choosing, wholly subject to the will and policy of a conqueror."

Well, would that be so bad? Is stopping Hitler from doing this worth the sacrifices of war?

> To the people of the Americas, a triumphant Hitler would say, as he said after the seizure of Austria, and as he said after Munich [the conference at which Britain and France effectively gave Hitler license to take part of Czechoslovakia], and as he said after the seizure of Czechoslovakia: "I am now completely satisfied. This is the last territorial readjustment I will seek." And he would of course add: "All we want is peace, friendship, and profitable trade relations with you in the New World." . . .
>
> No, I am not speculating about all this. I merely repeat what is already in the Nazi book of world conquest. They plan to treat the Latin American nations as they are now treating the Balkans. They plan then to strangle the United States of America and the Dominion of Canada.

We operate daily by speculation and prediction. If you put your heirloom vase at the very edge of the table, you can speculate—predict—that it will be knocked over and shattered. This is not an accomplished fact, but based on prior experience with items perched on the edges of tables, you decide to move your treasure closer to the center of the table. That is common sense.

FDR took a similar common-sense approach in declaring an unlimited national emergency and preparing for war. He painted a vivid picture of Hitler's recent actions. The pattern was unmistakable: conquest, followed by promises of no further conquest, followed by more conquest, followed by more promises. Any "speculation" made on the basis of this history was thus elevated beyond mere speculation—"I merely repeat what is already in the Nazi book of world conquest."

An effective leader bases speculation on the patterns formed by recent events, actions, and facts. In presenting such speculation, he anticipates the standard counterargument (*Yes, it* might *happen. But, then, it* might *not.*) by appealing to the same common sense that tells us a leopard does not change his spots.

PROVIDE RATIONAL HOPE

"For the first time since the Japanese and the Fascists and the Nazis started along their blood-stained course of conquest they now face the fact that superior forces are assembling against them."

—Ninth annual message to Congress, January 6, 1942

The early days, weeks, and months of World War II offered little enough hope for the United States and its beleaguered allies. In Europe, England, the last holdout among the Old World democracies, was threatened with invasion. In Asia and the Pacific the Japanese juggernaut had swallowed up one island, one nation after another. In his Fireside Chat of December 9, 1941, Roosevelt had himself admitted, "So far, the news has been all bad."

Faced with nothing but adversity, it is the leader's task to find credible, rational, realistic hope and to present that to those she leads. This does not mean "looking on the bright side" or insisting that others try to do so. What it does mean is identifying the steps, the route, by which the current challenge will be met and met successfully. The bad news is real. The hope must be real, too—even more emphatically so.

At this point, one month after Pearl Harbor, the president was far from having victories to report. But he could make the nation aware that forces and plans were in place to defeat the enemy, terrible as that enemy was:

> Plans have been laid here and in the other capitals for coordinated and cooperative action by all the United Nations—military action and economic action. Already we have established, as you know, unified command of land, sea, and air forces in the southwestern Pacific theater of war. There will be a continuation of conferences and consultations among military staffs, so that the plans and operations of each will fit into the general strategy designed to crush the enemy. We shall not fight isolated wars—each nation going its own way. These twenty-six nations are united—not in spirit and determination alone, but in the broad conduct of the war in all its phases.
>
> For the first time since the Japanese and the Fascists the Nazis started along their blood-stained course of conquest they now face the fact that superior forces are assembling against them. Gone forever are the days when the aggressors could attack and destroy their victims one by one without unity of resistance. We of the United Nations will so dispose our forces that we can strike at the common enemy wherever the greatest damage can be done him.
>
> The militarists of Berlin and Tokyo started this war. But the massed, angered forces of common humanity will finish it.

These were bold words, one month after Pearl Harbor and in the face of multiple defeats in the Pacific and in Europe, yet they were anything but empty words. They were promises built on a foundation of facts—the very substance of credible hope. FDR identified the one element that up to that point had been missing in the Allied prosecution of the war: unity and strength in numbers. So far Axis victory had depended on the ability to take on nations separately, to divide and conquer, to isolate one people from another. Unite, cooperate, and coordinate, and the enemy would be deprived of the single advantage he had enjoyed. Twenty-six nations, FDR explained, were now arrayed against the Axis. Yes, individually, these nations had suffered grave losses. But "for the first time," the enemy had to "face the fact that superior forces are assembling against them."

There was, then, a powerful new element in this war, and Roosevelt used it to bring hope, rational hope, to those who until then had known nothing but the bad news of defeat.

PROGRESS REPORT

"In recent months, the main tides of conflict have been running our way—but we could not and cannot be content merely to drift with this favorable tide."

> —Message to Congress on the progress of the war,
> September 17, 1943

Old-school autocratic leaders rarely deigned to report to those they led. The contract between leader and led was simple and one-sided: The leader made all the decisions and issued all the orders; the led obeyed, followed, and asked no questions.

Such a contract was never acceptable in a democracy and it has disappeared from most business organizations as well. Why? Most businesses sufficiently stodgy to insist on clinging to the one-way leadership model have themselves disappeared. Depriving leadership of the eyes, ears, minds, and imaginations of the members of the organization is a terribly inefficient way to run any enterprise.

So most leaders consider that one of their most important jobs is to share information with the organization. Among the most dynamic ways of sharing information is the progress report. Where the news is bad, the progress report can present a realistic picture of what is happening and what must be done to improve or correct the situation. Where the news is good, the progress report builds on the tried-and-true maxim that nothing succeeds like success. Most of the time the news is neither all good nor all bad, and that is when the progress report becomes most important.

Both critics and admirers of Franklin Roosevelt have pointed to his irrepressible optimism. Critics called it unrealistic, admirers inspirational. In fact FDR was almost invariably realistic but also optimistic. While he never let reality make his reports pessimistic, he was careful to keep his optimism from contributing to an unrealistic and destructive complacency. The concluding sentence of the opening paragraph of his September 17, 1943, report to Congress is typical of this balanced approach: "In recent months, the main tides of conflict have been running our way—but we could not and cannot be content merely to drift with this favorable tide."

The news he conveyed was good, but FDR refused to deliver it passively and, more important, refused to allow his listeners to accept it passively. The tide is going our way, but we cannot rely on the tide.

Anyone with an interest in and knowledge of World War II would do well to read this speech in its entirety. (It may be found in John Gabriel Hunt, ed., *The Essential Franklin Delano Roosevelt* [New York: Gramercy, 1995], pp. 269–79.) The report that is given—of the Italian campaign and of the significance of the ouster of Benito Mussolini; of the bombing campaign over Germany and against the oil refineries of Ploieşti, Romania; of the Soviets' progress on the eastern front; and of the "long and difficult fight" in Asia and the Pacific—is remarkably accurate and scrupulously honest. It is also incisive, delivering in brief compass the most relevant, telling, and useful facts.

FDR held back nothing significant but he did not let the facts speak entirely for themselves. He guided his audience to the interpretation he wanted them to reach: "We face, in the Orient, a long and difficult fight. We must be prepared for heavy losses in winning that fight. The power of Japan will not collapse until it has been literally pounded into the dust. It would be the utmost folly for us to try to pretend otherwise." Having said this to brace the people for further sacrifice, FDR continued: "Even so, if the future is tough for us, think what it is for General Tojo [the military dictator of Japan] and his murderous gang. They may look to the north, to the south, to the east, or to the west. They can see closing in on them, from all directions, the forces of retribution under the Generalissimo Chiang Kai-shek, General MacArthur, Admiral Nimitz, and Admiral Lord Mountbatten."

After several paragraphs detailing the losses the Allies had inflicted on Japan, Roosevelt looked to the future: "It goes almost without saying that when Japan surrenders, the United Nations [the Allies] will never again let her have authority over the islands which were mandated to her by the League of Nations."

A progress report requires a look backward, a picture of the present, and a glimpse of the future. Note the conspicuous absence of the word "if" and the equally conspicuous use of the word "when." In FDR's picture of the war, realistic as it is, the one element he did not permit to intrude was doubt as to the ultimate outcome.

OFFER THE FUTURE

"But—on Christmas Eve this year—I can say to you that at last we may look forward into the future with real, substantial confidence that, however great the cost, 'peace on earth, goodwill toward men' can be and will be realized and insured. This year I can say that. Last year I could not do more than express a hope. Today I express a certainty—though the cost may be high and the time may be long."

—Fireside Chat on the Teheran and Cairo conferences, December 24, 1943

Sometimes we demand a lot from our leaders. We ask them not merely to *plan for* the future, but to *tell us* the future. Is this an unreasonable demand?

No—and yes.

To invest a leader with omniscience is both foolish and dangerous, but to expect a leader to assess the past and present and using this assessment, to make plausible predictions about the future is hardly unreasonable. It is asking a leader to do her job.

The value in the here and now of a prediction is the degree to which it seems convincingly founded in present reality. In his Fireside Chat relating two key conferences with Allied leaders, Josef Stalin, Winston Churchill, and Chiang Kai-shek, President Roosevelt began by making the new present reality of Christmas

Eve, 1943, vividly apparent to Americans. He reported that one year earlier, 1.7 million troops were serving overseas. "Today, this figure has been more than doubled to 3.8 million on duty overseas." Then he looked to the immediate future: "By next July 1, that number overseas will rise to over 5 million men and women." Such figures were impressive, but FDR leaped beyond them to present a vision that is almost miraculous to contemplate:

> That this is truly a world war was demonstrated to me when arrangements were being made with our overseas broadcasting agencies for the time to speak today to our soldiers, sailors, marines, and merchant seamen in every part of the world. In fixing the time for this broadcast, we took into consideration that at this moment here in the United States, and in the Caribbean and on the northeast coast of South America, it is afternoon. In Alaska and in Hawaii and the mid-Pacific, it is still morning. In Iceland, in Great Britain, in North Africa, in Italy and the Middle East, it is now evening.
>
> In the Southwest Pacific, in Australia, in China and Burma and India, it is already Christmas Day. So we can correctly say that at this moment, in those Far Eastern parts where Americans are fighting, today is tomorrow.

By this poetic and visionary—but entirely real—observation, Roosevelt segued into the future and he offered a prediction:

> But—on Christmas Eve this year—I can say to you that at last we may look forward into the future with real, substantial confidence that, however great the cost, 'peace on earth, goodwill toward men' can be and will be realized and insured. This year I can say that. Last year I could not do more than express a hope. Today I express a certainty—though the cost may be high and the time may be long.

It is easy for a leader to say "things will be better someday." It is not easy, however, to express this as "a certainty." FDR gave his inspiring vision of the future credibility by comparing the present with the past. A year ago the reality allowed only a "hope." Today, it permitted a "certainty." The rest of this Fireside Chat was devoted to a report on the combined and coordinated efforts of the United States and its allies. The report did not express a mere hope of ultimate success but a certainty, a certainty FDR undergirded with simple mathematics: "Britain, Russia, China, and the United States and their allies represent more than three-quarters of the total population of the earth."

The great message of this Fireside Chat was not just one of victory through international unity—although that *was* part of the message—but, on Christmas Eve, it was also a vision of a future beyond this particular war. The Teheran and Cairo conferences not only concerned war strategy, but a strategy for the world *after* the war. The conferences planted the seeds of a United Nations: "Britain, Russia, China, and the United States and their allies represent more than three-quarters of the total population of the earth. As long as these four nations with great military power stick together in determination to keep the peace there will be no possibility of an aggressor nation arising to start another world war." Even Germany and Japan were not beyond future redemption: "If the people of Germany and Japan are made to realize thoroughly that the world is not going to let them breakout again, it is possible, and, I hope, probable, that they will abandon their philosophy of aggression—the belief that they can gain the whole world even at the risk of losing their own souls."

On Christmas Eve, 1943, America was prepared to envision victory, but it took bold leadership indeed to guide the people beyond even this vision, to a world of "peace on earth, goodwill toward men."

Appendix

AN FDR CHRONOLOGY

1882	Born, January 30
1896–1900	Attends Groton School
1900–1904	Attends Harvard University
1905	Marries Eleanor Roosevelt, March 17
1907	Leaves Columbia University Law School to begin practicing law with a Wall Street firm
1910	Successfully runs for New York state senator
1912	Campaigns on behalf of Woodrow Wilson for president
1913–20	Serves as assistant secretary of the Navy
1917–18	United States fights in World War I
1920	Runs for vice president on the unsuccessful Cox ticket
1921	Contracts polio; becomes paraplegic
1924	Creates the Warm Springs Foundation to aid polio victims
1924	Gains national attention for speech nominating Al Smith as Democratic presidential candidate
1928	Elected New York governor; introduces pioneering social reforms and relief measures
1929	Great Depression begins
1930	Reelected New York governor
1932	As Democratic presidential nominee, promises the nation a "New Deal"

1932   Elected thirty-second president of the United States over incumbent Herbert Hoover

1933   During his first hundred days in office, introduces precedent-shattering Depression relief measures

1935   Social Security Administration created

1936   Elected to second term

1939   Germany invades Poland, September 1, beginning World War II

1939   At the urging of FDR, U.S. neutrality is altered to favor Britain and France against Germany, November 4

1940   Elected to third term; unprecedented in U.S. history

1941   Signs Lend-Lease Act, March 11, to aid Allied powers

1941   Japanese attack Pearl Harbor, December 7

1941   Delivers "day of infamy" speech; U.S. declares war, December 8

1942   U.S. Navy defeats Japanese at Battle of Midway, June 3–6; turning point of the Pacific war

1944   D-Day invasion begins, June 6; beginning of major Allied offensive in Europe

1945   Meets with Churchill and Stalin at Yalta, February 4–11

1945   Dies in Warm Springs, Georgia, April 12; Harry S. Truman becomes president

1945   Germany surrenders, May 7

1945   Japan surrenders, August 15; World War II ends

Recommended Reading

Alsop, Joseph. *FDR*. New York: Gramercy Books, 1982.

Blum, John Morton. *V Was for Victory: Politics and American Culture During World War II*. New York: Harvest/Harcourt Brace Jovanovich, 1976.

Burns, James MacGregor. *Roosevelt: The Lion and the Fox*. New York: Harcourt Brace Jovanovich, 1956.

————. *Roosevelt: The Soldier of Freedom*. New York: Harcourt Brace Jovanovich, 1970.

Burns, James MacGregor, and Susan Dunn. *The Three Roosevelts: Patrician Leaders Who Transformed America*. New York: Atlantic Monthly Press, 2001.

Casey, Steven. *Cautious Crusade: Franklin D. Roosevelt, American Public Opinion, and the War against Nazi Germany*. New York: Oxford University Press, 2001.

Cook, Blanche Wiesen. *Eleanor Roosevelt, 1884–1933*. New York: Viking, 1992.

————. *Eleanor Roosevelt: The Defining Years, 1933–1938*. New York: Viking, 1999.

Dallek, Robert. *Franklin D. Roosevelt and American Foreign Policy, 1932–1945*. Oxford University Press, 1979.

Davis, Kenneth S. *FDR: The Beckoning of Destiny, 1882–1928: A History*. New York: G.P. Putnam's Sons, 1971.

————. *FDR: The New Deal Years 1933–1937*. New York: Random House, 1986.

————. *FDR: The War President, 1940–1943*. New York: Random House, 2000.

Fleming, Thomas. *The New Dealers' War: FDR and the War within World War II*. New York: Basic Books, 2001.

Freidel, Frank. *Franklin D. Roosevelt: A Rendezvous with Destiny.* Boston: Little, Brown, 1990.

Gallagher, Hugh Gregory. *FDR's Splendid Deception.* New York: Dodd, Mead and Company, 1985.

Goodwin, Doris Kearns. *No Ordinary Time: Franklin and Eleanor Roosevelt, The Home Front in World War II.* Reprint ed., New York: Touchstone, 1995.

Grafton, John, ed. *Franklin Delano Roosevelt: Great Speeches.* Mineola, New York: Dover Publications, 1999.

Graham, Otis L., Jr., and Meghan Robinson Wander. *Franklin D. Roosevelt, His Life and Times: An Encyclopedia View.* Boston: G.K. Hall and Co., 1985.

Heinrichs, Waldo. *Threshold of War: Franklin D. Roosevelt and American Entry into World War II.* New York: Oxford University Press, 1988.

Hunt, John Gabriel, ed. *The Essential Franklin Delano Roosevelt.* New York: Gramercy Books, 1995.

Kimball, Warren F. *The Juggler: Franklin Roosevelt as Wartime Statesman.* Princeton, New Jersey: Princeton University Press, 1991.

Larrabee, Eric. *Commander in Chief: Franklin Delano Roosevelt, His Lieutenants, and Their War.* New York: Harper and Row, 1987.

Lash, Joseph P. *Eleanor and Franklin.* New York: W. W. Norton and Company, Inc., 1971.

Leuchtenburg, William E. *Franklin D. Roosevelt and the New Deal: 1932–1940.* New York: Harper and Row, 1963.

Maney, Patrick J. *The Roosevelt Presence: The Life and Legacy of FDR.* Reprint ed., Berkeley: University of California Press, 1998.

Parker, Stamford, ed. *FDR: The Words That Reshaped America.* New York: HarperCollins Quill, 2000.

Parrish, Thomas. *Roosevelt and Marshall: Partners in Politics and War.* New York: William Morrow and Company, Inc., 1989.

Schlesinger, Arthur M. Jr. *The Coming of the New Deal.* Boston: Houghton Mifflin Company, 1959.

Sherwood, Robert E. *Roosevelt and Hopkins: An Intimate History.* New York: Harper Brothers, 1948.

Ward, Geoffrey C. *Before the Trumpet: Young Franklin Roosevelt, 1882–1905.* New York: Harper and Row, 1985.

———. *A First-Class Temperament: The Emergence of Franklin Roosevelt.* New York: Harper Perennial, 1989.

Index